SQE 1 PREP COURSE

Constitutional and Administrat-ive Law

BY ANASTASIA & ANDREW VIALICHKA

First Edition

Published by MetExam
https://metexam.co.uk

(m)etexam

ISBN: 978-1-917053-01-3

ISBN: 978-1-917053-21-1(Hardcover)

The information provided in this book is subject to change without notice and should not be construed as a commitment by the authors or the publisher. While every effort has been made to ensure the accuracy of the information contained herein, the authors and publisher assume no responsibility for any errors or omissions, or for damages resulting from the use of the information contained in this book.

This publication is designed exclusively for educational purposes, serving as a comprehensive study aid for individuals preparing for the SQE 1 examination. It should not be construed as offering legal advice or as an authoritative resource on legal matters. Its primary objective is to facilitate learning and exam preparation.

Authors: Vialichka, Anastasia; Vialichka, Andrew
Title: Constitutional and Administrative Law. SQE 1 Prep Course / Anastasia Vialichka, Andrew Vialichka.
Description: First Edition. | London: MetExam, 2024.
Identifiers: ISBN 978-1-917053-01-3
Subjects: LCSH Constitutional law—United Kingdom—Examinations, questions, etc. | Administrative law—United Kingdom—Examinations, questions, etc. | Constitutional law—England—Examinations, questions, etc. | Administrative law—Wales—Examinations, questions, etc. | Legal education—United Kingdom. | Legal education—England. | Legal education—Wales.

INTRODUCTION

Welcome to the threshold of your legal career in England and Wales. This guide is an integral part of the MetExam series, meticulously designed to equip you for the Solicitors Qualifying Examination (SQE 1). Here, you will embark on a journey through the complexities of Constitutional and Administrative Law and EU Law, gaining crucial insights and tools vital for your success.

This introduction is more than a starting point; it is a comprehensive roadmap designed to lay a solid foundation for your legal education. It aims to arm you with the intellectual rigour required to meet the legal profession's challenges and emerge as a knowledgeable, skilled solicitor.

Embrace this educational journey with enthusiasm and dedication. Allow this guide to be your constant companion and mentor as you navigate the path towards legal mastery and professional excellence.

Throughout this text, authors draw upon a wealth of legal scholarship and case law. While specific contributions are not cited in the body of the book, a comprehensive list of all works referenced can be found at the end. These references serves as an acknowledgment of the significant works that have informed this text and as a resource for readers seeking to explore the subject matter further.

CHAPTER 1. CONSTITU-TION

1. Overview of Constitution

A constitution comprises the fundamental principles or established precedents that form the legal basis for a nation's governance.

It typically serves to:

(a) **Establish** and delineate the core structures of the state, including the legislative, executive, and judicial branches;

(b) **Define** the scope of authority and interaction between the legislative, executive, and judicial branches; and

(c) **Govern** the interactions between the state, its governing bodies, and the citizens.

This text will guide you through the foundational constitutional principles that govern these functions within the UK, offering a foundational understanding of UK constitutional law.

2. The UK's Unwritten Constitution

The UK stands alongside a handful of nations globally without a codified constitution.

An unwritten, or more accurately, an uncodified constitution does not have a single, consolidated written document that outlines its most critical laws.

This contrasts with nations like the United States, Australia, or South Africa, each of which possesses a formal document titled 'The Constitution' that clearly enunciates the most significant legal and governmental guidelines.

CHAPTER 2. CHARACTERISTICS OF THE BRITISH CONSTITUTION

1. Multiple Sources

Due to the absence of a singular, comprehensive document, the UK's constitutional provisions are found across various sources, encompassing both legal statutes and non-legal guidelines, which have emerged at different times throughout history. These sources comprise statutes passed by Parliament, principles established by common law, and traditional practices known as constitutional conventions.

Additionally, the European Convention on Human Rights, as incorporated by the Human Rights Act 1998, serves as a legal source.

From 1973 until the 31st of January 2020, the UK was part of the European Union ('EU'). In this period, EU legislation, under the auspices of the European Communities Act 1972, became a key element of UK law.

Following the UK's exit from the EU, there was an initial transitional phase until the 31st of December 2020, wherein EU laws were still applicable within the UK.

Subsequent to this transition, although most EU legislation has been retained in UK law, it is now referred to as 'retained EU law' as per the European Union (Withdrawal) Act 2018 and the European Union (Withdrawal Agreement) Act 2020.

2. Adherence to the Rule of Law

The principle of the rule of law is a cornerstone of the UK constitution, mandating that laws be enforced impartially, that governmental actions are grounded in law, and that laws should not be retrospective in their application.

The judiciary plays a crucial role in maintaining this principle.

3. Absence of constitutional entrenchment and the principle of parliamentary supremacy

Unlike the situation in nations with a formalised constitution, where the constitution is typically 'entrenched' and holds precedence as the highest law, the UK's constitution does not have this entrenched status. In countries with entrenched constitutions, any ordinary statutes that conflict with the constitution can be invalidated or overturned.

By contrast, the UK's legal hierarchy places Acts of Parliament at the apex. Due to the absence of an entrenched constitution, the ultimate authority is vested in Parliament itself—a concept referred to as parliamentary sovereignty or supremacy.

From this principle of parliamentary sovereignty, it follows that amending the constitution legally requires only a conventional Act of Parliament passed by a simple majority in both the House of Commons and the House of Lords.

Consequently, numerous constitutional rules are embodied within Acts of Parliament which, in principle, can be modified or repealed like any other law.

Examples of Acts of Parliament with constitutional implications include the following, many of which are discussed in later chapters.

(a) **Magna Carta 1297**—guaranteed certain legal protections, including the right to jury trial;

(b) **Bill of Rights 1689**—asserted the sovereignty of Parliament over the Monarch;

(c) **Act of Union 1706**—created the Union of Scotland and England, governed by one Parliament based at Westminster;

(d) **European Communities Act 1972**—gives effect to the UK's membership of the European Union;

(e) **Human Rights Act 1998**—incorporated rights protected by the European Convention on Human Rights into UK law;

(f) **Scotland Act 1998**—created the Scottish Parliament;

(g) **Constitutional Reform Act 2005**—created the Supreme Court and the procedure for appointments to the judiciary;

(h) **Fixed-term Parliaments Act 2011**—sets out in which circumstances a general election is held;

(i) **Succession to the Crown Act 2012**—modernised the line of succession to the throne;

(j) **European Union (Notification of Withdrawal) Act 2017**—enabled the government to notify the EU of the UK's intention to withdraw from the European Union; and

(k) **European Union (Withdrawal) Act 2018**—makes provision for the retention of EU law in UK law as 'retained EU law'.

4. Judicial Inability to Nullify Legislation

The UK constitution's lack of a formal entrenched status and the enduring doctrine of parliamentary sovereignty result in the courts having no authority to nullify an Act of Parliament on the grounds of it being 'unconstitutional'.

4.1 Issuing a Declaration of Incompatibility

The judiciary's approach to challenging legislation comes in the form of issuing a 'declaration of incompatibility'. Such a declaration indicates that a piece of legislation is not aligned with the rights safeguarded under the **Human Rights Act 1998.**

It's important to note that this declaration doesn't immediately alter the legal standing of the legislation in question; instead, it signals to Parliament that there may be a need for legislative adjustment.

5. The Role of Judiciary

Courts in the UK are often called upon to interpret constitutional legislation, such as Acts of Parliament.

When the relationship between two Acts or the extent of powers granted by legislation is ambiguous, it is the role of the courts to clarify and provide a decisive interpretation.

If Parliament finds the judicial interpretation of legislation unsatisfactory, it retains the power to revise the law to clarify its intent and content.

Development of Common Law:

Apart from statutory interpretation, the judiciary also shapes the constitution through the development of common law, which comprises legal principles established by court decisions.

The judiciary's role includes the articulation, refinement, and expansion of these principles, one of the most significant being the doctrines underpinning judicial review, further detailed later in this book.

6. The Role of Monarchy and Royal Prerogative in the UK Constitution

The UK is characterised as a constitutional monarchy, which implies that the Monarch's role and powers are defined by the constitution. Although the Monarch is legally endowed with significant powers, these are largely ceremonial in practice, with real political power being exercised by elected officials.

The **royal prerogative**, an element of common law, comprises the powers traditionally held by the Crown.

While 'Royal' harkens back to when the Monarch directly exerted these powers, today, they are predominantly executed by the government. Although rooted in common law, the royal prerogative **can be curtailed or modified** by an Act of Parliament.

Over time, many prerogative powers have been superseded by statutory provisions. The details and current status of the royal prerogative will be discussed more thoroughly in later sections.

The Ram Doctrine and 'Third Source' Powers:

The Ram Doctrine, sometimes referred to as 'Third Source' powers, recognises governmental powers that exist beyond statutory authority and the royal prerogative.

These are incidental powers assumed by the government to manage the day-to-day functions that are not specifically outlined by statute or by royal prerogative. These powers are essential for the government to perform its routine duties and are considered inherent to the operation of a sovereign government.

7. The Role of Constitutional Convention

Constitutional conventions constitute a fundamental, though unwritten, aspect of the UK's constitutional framework. These conventions are practices that, although not legally enforceable, have become an accepted part of political operations. They serve to fill the gaps where neither statute nor case law provides guidance.

For example, while the legal authority to appoint a Prime Minister resides with the Monarch, in practice, this is directed by a set of constitutional conventions which dictate that the Monarch must appoint the leader of the political party that has the confidence of the House of Commons.

These conventions emerge from historical precedents and are sustained by a sense of obligation to uphold them and the understanding that there is a constitutional rationale behind these practices. They are adhered to largely due to the political repercussions that may arise from not doing so.

Nevertheless, debates may occur over whether a convention is relevant to a particular circumstance, or if it has been adhered to or breached, as such matters can often be subject to interpretation and political judgement.

For instance, the convention that the House of Lords should not block a budget passed by the House of Commons is a principle established through tradition rather than law. This convention was solidified after the constitutional crisis of 1911, when the Lords rejected the People's Budget proposed by the Commons, leading to the Parliament Act 1911 which restricted the Lords' power to veto money bills.

In the contemporary setting, imagine a situation where the House of Commons passes a controversial budget that significantly raises taxes. Although the House of Lords might strongly disagree with the content of the budget and might technically have the power to reject it, they would typically abstain from doing so because of the constitutional convention that dictates they should not obstruct the Commons' control over financial legislation.

This reflects the respect for the democratic principle that elected representatives in the Commons have the final say on financial matters.

Other **Notable Constitutional Conventions:**

(a) **Ministerial Accountability:** There is a convention that government ministers must resign if they are personally responsible for serious errors or misconduct.

(b) **Legislative Consent:** The UK Parliament generally does not legislate on matters that have been devolved to Scotland, Wales, or Northern Ireland without the consent of the respective devolved legislature, adhering to the Sewel Convention.

(c) **Prime Ministerial Advice:** It is customary for the Monarch to act on the advice of the Prime Minister in government matters.

(d) **Ministerial Appointments:** Ministers typically must be members of one of the two Houses of Parliament and are appointed by the Monarch on the recommendation of the Prime Minister.

(e) **Parliamentary Accountability:** The government owes its accountability to Parliament, with ministers required to appear in Parliament, respond to questions, and participate in debates.

These conventions are not codified but are documented and explained in various government documents such as the Cabinet Manual and the Ministerial Code, which serve as operational guides for members of the government.

8. The United Kingdom: A Union State with Devolved Powers

The United Kingdom, while retaining parliamentary sovereignty at its core, has evolved into a state that practises devolution, delegating powers to Scotland, Wales, and Northern Ireland. This devolution is asymmetric, with each of the nations having different scopes of power.

England, lacking its own legislature, is directly governed by the UK Parliament, where laws may be made that apply to England alone or to all four nations together.

(a) **Union State:** The UK is composed of four nations but is not a federal system like the United States; instead, it remains a union state with a centralised government that has ultimate legislative authority.

(b) **Three Jurisdictions:** England and Wales share a legal jurisdiction, while Scotland and Northern Ireland each have their own. UK Parliament has the authority to legislate for all three but typically respects the autonomy of devolved powers.

(c) **Devolved Powers:** Devolution has provided Scotland, Wales, and Northern Ireland with their own legislative bodies and varying degrees of autonomy to make decisions on local matters, such as education, health, and transportation.

The relationship between the centralised UK government and the devolved administrations is dynamic and has been subject to political negotiations, particularly in light of Brexit and other constitutional debates.

9. Parliamentary Framework and Governance

The governance structure of the UK is anchored in a parliamentary system, distinct from a presidential system seen in countries like France or the USA.

Here's an overview of its features:

(a) **Integrated Leadership:** The heads of the government, including the Prime Minister and other ministers, are drawn from the legislature, integrating the executive and legislative branches.

(b) **Legislative Dual Role:** Members of Parliament (MPs) have a dual role: they are part of the legislative body and potentially part of the executive government if selected as ministers.

(c) **Government Formation:** The government is formed as a result of parliamentary elections. The political party or coalition with a majority in the House of Commons typically forms the government, and its leader becomes the Prime Minister.

(d) **Prime Minister Selection:** Unlike a presidential system where the head of government is elected directly by the people, the UK Prime Minister is usually the leader of the majority party in the House of Commons and is formally appointed by the Monarch.

(e) **Accountability to Parliament:** The government is accountable to Parliament, especially the House of Commons. It must retain the confidence of the majority of MPs to stay in power. If it loses a vote of confidence, it may trigger a general election or the formation of a new government.

This parliamentary system promotes a different dynamic of political accountability and integration between the executive and legislative functions, often resulting in a system where policy and administration are more closely connected to legislative approval and support.

CHAPTER 3. FUNDA-MENTAL PRINCIPLES UNDERPINNING THE CONSTITUTION

The multifaceted sources of the UK constitution uphold numerous cardinal principles that fundamentally shape and define its structure and character.

Three pivotal principles underpin the UK constitution:

(a)   **the separation of powers**

(b)   **the rule of law**

(c)   **parliamentary sovereignty.**

While these principles are cornerstones of the constitutional framework, they can, at times, intersect and potentially conflict when applied to their extremes. The ensuing sections delve into these principles, exploring their interplay and the delicate balance that defines the governance and legal structure of the UK.

1. The Primacy of Parliamentary Sovereignty

Parliamentary sovereignty is the bedrock principle of the United Kingdom's constitutional framework. It enshrines the preeminence of Parliament in the legal hierarchy, establishing it as the apex law-making authority within the UK. This principle manifests in three fundamental tenets:

(a) **Firstly,** Parliament possesses the unrestricted legal authority to legislate, amend, or repeal any law.

(b) **Secondly,** there exists no entity or individual with the jurisdiction to invalidate or supersede legislation enacted by Parliament.

(c) **Lastly,** the principle of continuity and renewal is intrinsic to parliamentary sovereignty, meaning that no Parliament can impose limitations on the legislative powers of its successors.

Collectively, these elements affirm the absolute legislative supremacy of Acts of Parliament within the UK's legal system.

1.1 The Unbounded Legislative Authority of Parliament

The legislative supremacy of the UK Parliament allows it to craft laws on any conceivable subject, without restrictions on the scope or nature of the legislation it enacts. This means Parliament holds the power to pass laws on any topic, no matter how controversial or peculiar they may be, such as hypothetically legislating to harm blue-eyed infants or to regulate activities in a foreign city like Paris.

(a) **Self-Definition and Adaptation.** Parliament holds the unique ability to redefine its structure and processes by enacting new laws. This self-modifying capability enables Parliament to adapt and evolve through its own legislative instruments.

The conventional route for a bill to become law involves its passage through both Houses of Parliament and culminating with the Monarch's Royal Assent. However, under the unique provisions of the Parliament Acts 1911 and 1949, a bill can become law with the approval of the House of Commons alone, circumventing the House of Lords entirely.

Judicial interpretation upholds that such Acts, even without the concurrence of the House of Lords, are fully legitimate Acts of Parliament, indistinguishable in legal status from those passed via the customary legislative process.

(b) **Parliament's Position on International Agreements.** In the domestic sphere, international treaties ratified by the UK don't automatically become part of UK law. For international agreements to take effect domestically, they must be transposed into UK law by way of parliamentary enactment, thus affirming the principle that legal obligations on an international level must be explicitly accepted and integrated by Parliament to have internal legal impact.

When the United Kingdom ratified the United Nations Convention on Contracts for the International Sale of Goods (CISG), it undertook certain obligations on an international level to adhere to rules facilitating international trade.

However, without specific legislative action, the provisions of the CISG would not apply to contracts within the UK. To give domestic effect to the CISG, Parliament would need to pass an Act incorporating the treaty's provisions into the UK legal system, thereby making them enforceable in UK courts.

(c) **Extraterritorial Legislative Reach.** The UK Parliament can extend the jurisdiction of its laws beyond the nation's geographic confines, exerting legal influence or control in international or extra-territorial contexts.

The UK's Bribery Act 2010 has wide-ranging implications for UK businesses operating internationally. It holds that a UK corporation or individual can be held accountable for bribery offences committed anywhere in the world, as long as they have a connection to the UK.

This means that a British company found to be involved in corrupt practices overseas may face prosecution back in the UK, even if the actions occurred in countries with different legal standards regarding bribery.

(d) **Retroactive Legislative Power.** While it is standard for legislative bodies to enact laws with a forward-looking perspective, Parliament is also vested with the capacity to legislate retroactively. This means it can pass laws that alter the legal status of actions after they have occurred. Such retrospective legislation can convert previously lawful actions into unlawful ones, which raises significant considerations concerning the rule of law, as it touches on the principles of legal certainty and predictability. These issues are explored in depth in subsequent sections of this discussion.

1.2 The Inviolability of Parliamentary Acts

The principle that no individual or entity has the authority to nullify Acts of Parliament underscores the negative facet of parliamentary sovereignty. This principle asserts that even if legislation is deemed morally reprehensible or fundamentally flawed, the judiciary lacks the jurisdiction to nullify or 'strike down' such Acts. The judiciary has acknowledged that the legislative reach of Parliament encompasses the authority to enact laws that could be characterised as 'unconstitutional.'

It's critical to recognise that Acts of Parliament stand as the apex of legal authority, rendering any judicial attempt to invalidate them as contrary to the doctrine of parliamentary supremacy or sovereignty. On the Solicitors Qualifying Examination (SQE), any suggestion that a court can nullify an Act of Parliament should be immediately recognised as incorrect.

However, the seemingly absolute power of Parliament is moderated by two significant checks: public sentiment and judicial interpretation.

(a) **Public Mandate.** Considering that the House of Commons is a body of elected representatives, any MP involved in passing legislation deemed egregious is likely to face electoral repercussions in subsequent elections.

(b) Judicial Interpretation. Another pivotal role of the judiciary is the interpretation of statutes. Courts operate under the presumption that Parliament's legislative intentions align with the rule of law, prompting a judicious interpretation of statutes to reflect this principle.

If a statute stipulates that a decision by a statutory body is beyond judicial scrutiny, the courts may interpret this to mean that only decisions made within the lawful authority of the body are protected from challenge.

This interpretation permits judicial review of the body's decisions to ensure they comply with the law, thereby maintaining the rule of law and the ability to question the legality of governmental actions.

(c) The Enrolled Bill Doctrine. This principle has practical implications, one of which is the court's non-interference with the legislative validity. According to the Enrolled Bill Doctrine, once an Act has been duly passed by both Houses of Parliament and has received Royal Assent, the judiciary will uphold the Act without contest. The term 'enrolled bill' refers to the formal ledger of legislation ratified by Parliament, which the courts would theoretically reference when assessing an Act's legitimacy.

The Enrolled Bill Doctrine further stipulates that the courts abstain from scrutinising the parliamentary procedures that led to an Act's enactment. Thus, should any procedural anomalies occur during the legislative process in either the House of Commons or House of Lords, the enacted statute remains legally effective. This notion extends to the concept of parliamentary privilege, which safeguards the procedural autonomy of both Houses from judicial scrutiny.

A party in a legal case may claim that a particular piece of legislation should be disregarded because it was passed during an uncommon late-night session in the House of Commons, which they argue compromised the quality of debate and scrutiny.

However, as per the Enrolled Bill Rule, the court would not entertain this argument. The court's role is not to evaluate the circumstances or procedures under which Parliament passed an Act; if the Act appears on the official roll of legislation, it is considered valid and is to be applied as such, irrespective of the internal processes that led to its enactment.

1.3 The Principle of Non-Binding Successive Parliaments

A fundamental tenet of parliamentary sovereignty is that no parliament can create laws that will irreversibly bind future parliaments. This means that any legislative body has the capacity to overturn or modify the laws established by its predecessors. This can occur in two distinct manners: through express repeal or implied repeal.

(a) **Express Repeal.** In an express repeal, the legislation explicitly specifies which Acts of Parliament, or portions thereof, are to be rescinded or annulled. This direct approach leaves no ambiguity as to which laws have been withdrawn.

(b) **Implied Repeal.** Implied repeal occurs when Parliament enacts a new law that addresses the same subject matter as an existing one, leading to an inconsistency between the two. Although the newer law does not directly repeal the older one, the conflict necessitates a choice between them. In these situations, the judiciary will uphold the more recent legislation, based on the assumption that the latest Act reflects the current intentions of Parliament.

Consider a situation where the UK Parliament enacted a law in 2005 mandating specific safety standards for electrical appliances.

Then, in 2020, new legislation concerning the same domain of electrical safety was passed but with different, perhaps more stringent, standards. If discrepancies arise between the two sets of standards, the latter law would supersede the former, effectively implying the repeal of the earlier provisions that are at odds with the new standards.

1.4 The Impact of EU Membership on Parliamentary Sovereignty

The UK's historical involvement with the European Union (EU) presented a unique interplay with the principle of parliamentary sovereignty. This relationship was chiefly mediated through the European Communities Act 1972 (ECA 1972), which effectively wove EU law into the fabric of UK legal systems. The ECA 1972 stipulated that any binding EU legislation would be automatically assimilated into UK law, thereby negating the need for any additional legislative processes.

(a) **The Supremacy of EU Law.** The principle of EU law's supremacy meant that it took precedence over conflicting national laws across all member states, including the UK. This was operationalised within the UK through the ECA 1972. In instances where UK law clashed with EU law, UK courts would set aside the conflicting domestic law. This practice was based on the understanding that the British Parliament had willingly curtailed its sovereignty by enacting the ECA 1972.

(b) **Reconciling EU Law with Acts of Parliament.** When faced with inconsistencies between EU law and Acts of Parliament, the judiciary in the UK was tasked with the disapplication of the conflicting Act. This was not seen as a contravention of UK law but rather as adherence to it, under the premise that EU law was to take precedence over

UK legislation as per the ECA 1972's mandates. This approach maintained the legal integrity of both EU law and the principle of parliamentary sovereignty within the context of the UK's EU membership.

2. The Principle of the Separation of Powers in the UK

The doctrine of the separation of powers posits that there are three main branches of government—the executive, the legislature, and the judiciary—each with distinct functions and personnel. This doctrine is instrumental in preventing the concentration of power by ensuring that each branch serves as a check on the others, thereby promoting accountability and safeguarding liberty.

In the context of the UK's constitutional framework, this principle is observed with some nuances:

(a) **The Executive:** This branch comprises the Government, including the Prime Minister and other ministers, who are responsible for the day-to-day administration of the state, the implementation of laws, and policy-making.

(b) **The Legislature:** Known as Parliament in the UK, this branch is responsible for creating laws and consists of two Houses—the House of Commons and the House of Lords. Members of the Government (executive) are typically drawn from the legislature, which is a departure from a strict interpretation of the separation of powers.

(c) **The Judiciary:** This independent branch interprets the law and adjudicates disputes. In the UK, judicial independence is maintained through various means, including security of tenure for judges and the doctrine of judicial review, which allows the judiciary to oversee the legality of executive actions.

Although the Monarch is historically the source of all three powers, their contemporary role in legislative and judicial matters is largely ceremonial, with actual power being exercised by Parliament and the judiciary.

2.1 The Legislative Branch of the UK

In the United Kingdom, the legislative branch, which is tasked with creating laws, is embodied by Parliament. The UK Parliament operates as a bicameral institution, consisting of two distinct chambers:

(a) **The House of Commons.** This chamber is composed of Members of Parliament (MPs) who are elected by the public. The House of Commons holds significant authority in the legislative process, including financial matters and the scrutinising of government activities.

(b) **The House of Lords.** Unlike the House of Commons, the House of Lords is not an elected body. It includes life peers, bishops, and hereditary peers. Although it cannot ultimately block legislation, it plays a critical role in reviewing and revising proposed laws.

In addition to the UK Parliament, there are devolved legislative bodies within the United Kingdom with circumscribed powers over certain policy areas. These are:

(a) **The Scottish Parliament.** Responsible for various matters specific to Scotland, such as education and health, it has the power to legislate within the confines of its devolved competencies.

(b) **The Welsh Parliament (Senedd Cymru).** It has legislative authority in areas that have been devolved to Wales, including health services and local government.

(c) **The Northern Ireland Assembly.** It holds legislative powers over certain areas specific to Northern Ireland, similar to the devolved powers of Scotland and Wales.

Each of these devolved institutions can enact legislation pertinent to their respective nations within the UK, operating under the constraints of their devolved powers and in harmony with the overarching sovereignty of the UK Parliament.

2.2 Executive

In the UK's constitutional framework, the executive branch is charged with the duty of enforcing the laws established by the legislature and managing the country's day-to-day governance. This includes adhering to legislation passed by Parliament and wielding powers granted by the royal prerogative. The executive comprises the following:

(a) **The Government.** Led by the Prime Minister, the central government is composed of various ministers and their departments, each tasked with specific areas of public policy and administration.

(b) **Devolved Governments.** In Scotland, Wales, and Northern Ireland, devolved executives have the authority to govern in certain policy areas that have been transferred from the UK Parliament to the devolved legislatures. These areas can include education, health, and transportation, among others.

(c) **Local Councils and Mayors.** Across the UK, local councils serve as a tier of regional governance, responsible for local matters such as housing, planning, and community services. In some regions, directly elected mayors hold executive powers, providing leadership and making decisions on regional issues.

The executive operates within the constraints of the law as set by the national Parliament and is accountable to both the legislature and the public. Through its various levels and offices, the executive ensures that the nation's laws are put into practice and that public services meet the needs of citizens.

2.3 The Judicial Branch

Within the governance structure of the United Kingdom, the judiciary constitutes the network of courts and tribunals tasked with interpreting legislation and adjudicating disputes. At the apex of this structure sits the UK Supreme Court, serving as the ultimate arbiter in legal matters. Disputes subject to judicial scrutiny can arise between private parties; however, cases involving the state and individuals or disputes within state institutions hold particular constitutional significance.

Judges possess the authority to delineate the boundaries of power among various constitutional entities. A case in point is the judiciary's capability to determine whether the executive could utilise royal prerogative powers to initiate the UK's departure from the European Union or if such a significant step necessitated legislation passed by Parliament. Moreover, the judiciary functions as a guardian against executive overreach by employing the mechanism of judicial review. This legal process permits the examination and, where necessary, the challenge of the executive's actions in a court of law.

3. Principle of Legal Governance

The third foundational concept in the UK's constitutional framework is the principle of the rule of law. This principle dictates that the government's actions must be founded on legal authority. Consequently, it is the established law that governs, not the arbitrary decisions of those wielding power. It's essential to acknowledge that the rule of law is not absolute; rather, it serves as a guiding principle underpinning the legal system.

Although theoretically possible, the principle of parliamentary sovereignty could allow deviations from the rule of law's standards.

3.1 No Punishment Without Breach of Law

A fundamental aspect of the rule of law is that individuals should only face punishment if they have contravened an established law, and any such penalty must be administered in accordance with legal procedures.

This principle underscores the preference for legally defined parameters over discretionary power in government actions. Discretion can often result in decisions that are arbitrary or inequitable, undermining fair governance.

In contrast, when actions are regulated by clear legal directives, individuals have the opportunity to align their conduct with the law, thus upholding a society that is steered by due process and legal predictability.

For instance, if a government official issues a directive to search a citizen's home based on their political expressions without any legal foundation for such an action, such a directive would be deemed invalid. Legal authorisation is a prerequisite for such invasive actions, and its absence renders the directive a violation of the rule of law.

3.2 Equality Before the Law

The principle that no individual is exempt from the law is a cornerstone of the rule of law. This dictates that every person, regardless of their status, position, or power, is subject to the law's mandates and constraints.

In practice, this principle is largely upheld within the legal system; there have been instances where government officials, including ministers, have been held accountable under criminal law, similar to any other citizen.

The judiciary has also demonstrated its commitment to this principle by holding ministers accountable for legal violations, such as contempt of court, thus reinforcing the concept that the law is supreme and applies equally to all individuals.

For instance, consider a scenario where a Member of Parliament (MP) is found to have engaged in fraudulent financial activities. Despite their position and influence, the MP would be subject to the same legal proceedings and potential penalties as any other citizen found guilty of similar offences.

This example underscores the impartiality of the law, reinforcing the notion that all individuals, regardless of their role or status, are subject to the same legal standards and consequences.

3.3 Exception of Parliamentary Privilege

Parliamentary privilege stands as a notable exception to the principle of equal application of the law, providing certain immunities to Members of Parliament. Notably, comments made within the proceedings of Parliament are immune from legal challenge or judicial scrutiny, ensuring unfettered freedom of expression for MPs and Lords within the chambers.

This aspect of parliamentary privilege highlights a situation where the rule of law yields to other constitutional imperatives, demonstrating the dynamic balance between different constitutional principles within the UK's legal framework.

For instance, imagine an MP who, during a debate in the House of Commons, accuses a corporation of illegal environmental practices. If these allegations were made outside of Parliament, they might be subject to legal action for defamation. However, within the confines of parliamentary proceedings, the MP is protected by parliamentary privilege.

This means the corporation would be unable to sue the MP for defamation based on the statements made in the House. This principle is crucial for maintaining the independence and efficacy of Parliament, allowing MPs to speak and act without fear of legal repercussions, thus fostering open and robust debate on matters of public interest.

3.4 The Issue with Retrospective Legislation

Adherence to the rule of law typically entails a set of procedural standards that uphold legal fairness. One of the fundamental expectations derived from the rule of law is that laws should be applied prospectively, not retrospectively. Retrospective legislation is problematic because it applies to actions that occurred before the law was enacted, potentially criminalising actions that were lawful at the time they were taken.

This retrospective application can appear as a form of governance by fiat, undermining the very predictability and stability that the rule of law seeks to ensure. Consequently, retrospective laws may be perceived as arbitrary, conflicting with the principle that laws should enable individuals to align their conduct with legal expectations.

For instance, consider a situation where a new law is enacted, imposing additional tax liabilities on certain financial transactions that were executed two years prior to the law's enactment. The individuals and corporations involved in these transactions had complied with the tax laws as they existed at the time. However, with the retrospective application of the new law, they suddenly find themselves liable for additional taxes.

Such retrospective legislation can be perceived as unfair, as it penalises actions that were lawful at the time they were taken. It challenges the rule of law principle that laws should provide a stable and predictable framework for governing conduct, thereby allowing individuals and entities to plan their affairs with reasonable certainty about their legal obligations and rights.

3.5 Additional Aspects of the Rule of Law

The rule of law encompasses various additional principles which are crucial for its effective application:

(a) The law should be readily accessible to the public, and its provisions should be clear, comprehensible, and predictable to facilitate compliance.

(b) The law must afford mechanisms for resolving civil disputes without incurring excessive costs or encountering undue delays.

(c) The state's procedures for resolving disputes must be equitable, upholding principles of procedural fairness.

(d) There should be judicial oversight to ensure the enforcement and application of these principles is consistent and fair.

3.6 The Status of Fundamental Rights

Within the common law framework, certain rights are recognised as 'fundamental'. These rights underpin the rule of law, including the unassailable right to access the courts.

Moreover, the principle asserts that governmental and administrative decisions should adhere to an elemental standard of fairness.

It is established that these fundamental rights can only be curtailed or modified by Parliament through explicit legislative action. In the absence of clear statutory directives to the contrary, the judiciary will interpret laws in a way that honours these rights, thus demonstrating the complementary relationship between the rule of law and the sovereignty of Parliament.

A new policy introduced by a government agency restricts the availability of legal aid, making it virtually inaccessible for certain disadvantaged groups. This policy is challenged on the grounds that it violates the fundamental right to access the courts. Since the policy effectively bars a significant section of society from seeking legal redress due to financial constraints, it is viewed as infringing upon this basic right.

The courts, in reviewing this policy, would likely scrutinise whether there is explicit legislative authority that permits such a significant curtailment of the right to access justice. Absent clear legislative intent to limit this fundamental right, the courts would typically interpret the law in a way that aligns with the principle of ensuring fair and equal access to justice, thereby upholding the rule of law.

3.7 Human Rights Act 1998

Beyond the common law protections, the Human Rights Act 1998 plays a pivotal role in ensuring that UK legislation aligns with the spectrum of rights safeguarded by the Act. Where it is not feasible to interpret a piece of legislation in a manner that is consistent with these human rights, the judiciary has the authority to issue a 'declaration of incompatibility'.

This declaration serves as an advice to Parliament, highlighting potential human rights conflicts within the legislation. While Parliament frequently takes action to reconcile such discrepancies, the ultimate decision often lies with them, reflecting the enduring principle of parliamentary sovereignty.

3.8 The Role of Judicial Review

The judicial review process is a cornerstone of legal oversight in the UK, providing a mechanism to scrutinise the legality of public authority decisions. Rather than being an avenue for appealing the decisions themselves, judicial review focuses on the legal boundaries within which the decisions are made.

This process upholds both the principle of parliamentary sovereignty—by ensuring that authorities do not exceed the powers granted to them by Parliament—and the rule of law, by demanding that these powers are exercised within the legal framework established by legislation.

CHAPTER 4. PARLIAMENT'S CORE FUNCTIONS

1. Parliamentary Structure

1.1 The House of Commons

The House of Commons consists of 650 elected Members of Parliament (MPs), each representing a specific geographic constituency secured during the most recent general election. The majority of MPs are affiliated with a political party, and those belonging to the party currently in power are seated alongside the government, including ministers who occupy the prominent front benches.

The principal opposition party forms Her Majesty's Loyal Opposition, with its leader assuming the role of Leader of the Opposition. This individual engages in regular discourse with the Prime Minister, critiquing the government's performance. The Leader of the Opposition is assisted by the Shadow Cabinet, whose members are tasked with challenging and questioning their corresponding government ministers. For instance, the Shadow Foreign Secretary would directly engage with the Foreign Secretary on matters of foreign policy.

The Speaker of the House of Commons. The Speaker, elected by all MPs, is responsible for presiding over debates and upholding the rules of parliamentary conduct. To maintain neutrality, the Speaker relinquishes any party affiliations and operates in a non-partisan capacity.

1.2 The Election Process

Elections to the House of Commons, known as general elections, determine the composition of the legislature. In contrast, the House of Lords remains an appointed body without electoral processes. In the UK's parliamentary system, general elections fulfil a twofold purpose: they elect Members of Parliament and simultaneously decide which political party, or coalition of parties, is to form the government.

Ordinarily, the tenure of Parliament spans five years, at the end of which Parliament dissolves, MPs relinquish their seats, and a general election is convened.

The Fixed-term Parliaments Act 2011. The Fixed-term Parliaments Act 2011 stipulates that a general election can be triggered prior to the completion of the standard five-year term under **two specific conditions:**

(a) A **motion declaring** "This House has no confidence in Her Majesty's Government" is approved by the House of Commons, and subsequently, no motion affirming "This House has confidence in Her Majesty's Government" is passed within the next 14 days; or

(b) **At least two-thirds of the total number of MPs,** which equates to 434 out of 650, cast their votes in support of holding an early general election.

Moreover, by virtue of parliamentary sovereignty, Parliament retains the authority to enact new legislation that supersedes the Fixed-term Parliaments Act 2011, thereby setting an alternative date for the forthcoming election.

Imagine a situation where Parliament decides to amend the succession rules to implement gender-neutral succession, where the throne passes to the monarch's eldest child regardless of gender, or to introduce a rule where the monarch's role rotates among the countries of the United Kingdom. Such changes would significantly alter centuries-old traditions governing the monarchy.

To enact this, Parliament would need to pass a new Act, effectively amending or replacing the existing laws governing the line of succession. This legislation would require the standard legislative process: approval by both the House of Commons and the House of Lords, followed by the Royal Assent.

Once enacted, this new law would supersede the current rules, illustrating the power of Parliament to make or unmake any law, even those with deep-rooted historical and cultural significance. This example underscores the fundamental principle of parliamentary sovereignty in the UK legal system, highlighting its capacity to reshape even the most established constitutional elements.

Eligibility for Becoming an MP. In general, most individuals are eligible to stand as candidates in parliamentary elections. Nonetheless, specific groups are prohibited from becoming MPs, even if they win an election:

(a)   Individuals **younger than 18 years** of age;

(b)   **Non-Commonwealth citizens,** with the exception of Irish citizens, who are permitted to become MPs;

(c)   **Members of the House of Lords.**

Additionally, certain professions are precluded from MP membership to preserve the separation of powers, ensuring that those in the judiciary or executive do not concurrently legislate.

This includes:

- **Judges serving in high-ranking courts** such as the High Court, Court of Appeal, and Supreme Court;

- **Civil service personnel;**

- **Armed forces members;**

- **Police force officers;**

- **Legislators from non-Commonwealth countries** and Ireland, including the European Parliament, as outlined in the House of Commons Disqualification Act 1975.

By-Elections. Seats in the House of Commons may become vacant due to an MP's death or resignation. When this occurs, a by-election is organised in the relevant constituency to elect a replacement.

The Recall of MPs Act 2015. Under certain circumstances, an MP may be subject **to a recall:**

(a) If **convicted of a crime** leading to imprisonment;

(b) If **suspended from the House of Commons** for at least 10 days due to misconduct;

(c) If **found culpable of falsifying expenses claims.**

When such situations arise, the Speaker informs the affected constituency, initiating a recall petition. If over 10% of the electorate in the constituency sign this petition, a by-election is triggered. The MP has been effectively recalled to their constituency and may choose to stand in the by-election.

1.3 Composition of the House of Lords

The House of Lords, as the second chamber of Parliament, is distinctive in that its members are not elected. Its composition includes approximately 800 members who fall into one of four distinct categories.

(a) Hereditary Peers. These individuals inherit titles such as Duke, Earl, Viscount, or Baron, which traditionally pass through family lineage, typically to the eldest son. Although there is a substantial number of hereditary peers, only 92 have the privilege to sit in the House of Lords, a limitation set by the House of Lords Act 1999.

(b) Life Peers. Appointed directly by the Monarch upon the recommendation of the Prime Minister, life peers receive the title of Baron for their lifetime. Appointments are often reflective of the political party vote shares from the last general election, maintaining a semblance of political representation. The life peerage does not carry over after death, thus ensuring the House of Lords is predominantly composed of appointed members rather than hereditary ones.

(c) Lords Spiritual. This group consists of the 26 most senior bishops from the Church of England, known as the Lords Spiritual, who hold seats in the House of Lords.

(d) Law Lords. Before the establishment of the Supreme Court, Law Lords, officially titled as Lords of Appeal in Ordinary, were appointed for life and served as the highest appellate judges in the UK. While the judicial function of the House of Lords has been transferred to the Supreme Court, some of the Law Lords retain their seats.

2. Primary Legislation

2.1 The State Opening and the Queen's Address

The lifespan of a Parliament is traditionally capped at five years, segmented into distinct sessions typically lasting a year, commencing in May. The ceremonial inauguration of each parliamentary session is punctuated by the State Opening, where the Monarch delivers the King's/Queen's Speech. This key event features the Monarch articulating the government's planned legislative agenda for the upcoming session, effectively setting the government's priorities and intended policies.

The timing of a parliamentary session is crucial for the progression of legislation. A bill must successfully navigate through the House of Commons and the House of Lords and subsequently be granted Royal Assent within the same session of its introduction. Failure to complete this legislative journey within the allotted time frame results in the bill's expiration, necessitating reintroduction in the subsequent session.

However, provisions exist for a bill to be 'carried over' to the next session by parliamentary consent, allowing the bill to pick up where it left off.

Between sessions, Parliament is in recess, putting a pause on all parliamentary activities until the next session's initiation. This interval underscores the procedural rhythms of the UK's legislative machinery.

2.2 The Curtailment of Parliament: Prorogation

The transition between parliamentary sessions is marked by prorogation, a formal mechanism initiated by the Monarch on the Prime Minister's counsel. This process brings one session to a close and signals the commencement of the next. Prorogation has the effect of temporarily suspending parliamentary proceedings, including all pending legislative business, which must either conclude before this suspension or resume in the following session if carried over.

The prerogative power to prorogue carries significant potential for misuse, as an extensive or unjustified prorogation could disrupt the legislative function and democratic process. Such an act would essentially halt Parliament's operations and could be construed as an attempt to circumvent parliamentary scrutiny.

To guard against abuse, any prorogation extending beyond a brief interlude necessitates a compelling justification. If deemed excessive and lacking reasonable grounds, such prorogation may face judicial scrutiny and potential annulment, affirming the judiciary's role in upholding constitutional propriety.

Consider a scenario where a new healthcare reform bill is introduced in the House of Commons on 10th June and successfully passes its Second Reading on 20th June. The detailed examination of the bill, known as the Committee Stage, is scheduled to begin on 30th June. Unexpectedly, the government announces the prorogation of Parliament on 25th June, with the subsequent session set to begin on 5th July, marked by the Queen's Speech.

In this situation, unless specific provisions are made to 'carry over' the bill, it would lapse due to the prorogation. The bill, therefore, would need to be reintroduced in the new session post-5th July, starting once again from the initial stages of the legislative process. This example highlights the significance of prorogation in shaping the legislative agenda and the potential implications for ongoing parliamentary proceedings.

2.3 The Procedure for Enacting Legislation

The journey of a bill through Parliament is a well-defined process, with both the House of Commons and the House of Lords following a similar sequence of stages. Typically, legislation proposed by the government is presented initially in the House of Commons. However, bills that are less contentious may commence their legislative passage in the House of Lords.

The progression of a bill encompasses several key stages:

(a) **First Reading.** This initial phase formally introduces the bill to the parliamentary chamber. It is purely procedural, entailing no debate, and serves to make the bill's text and its accompanying explanatory notes public.

(b) **Second Reading.** This stage provides the first opportunity for the principles and underlying purpose of the bill to be discussed. All Members of Parliament may engage in this debate, voicing support or raising objections.

(c) **Deliberation at the Committee Stage.** At the committee stage, the bill is examined with great attention to detail. Members of Parliament are presented with the opportunity to propose changes or amendments to the bill, which are then subject to rigorous debate and potential adoption into the bill's framework. The committee stage takes on one of **two primary forms:**

  • **Public Bill Committee.** A Public Bill Committee, comprising between 16 and 30 MPs, is established to undertake a thorough review of the bill. The committee's composition reflects the proportional distribution of the political parties within the main chamber. This committee has the authority to solicit and scrutinise evidence from specialists or advocacy groups relevant to the bill.

- **Committee of the Whole House.** For bills that are either non-contentious or demand urgent attention, or for those that carry significant constitutional weight, the Committee of the Whole House is convened. Although it operates as a committee, it assembles within the main Commons chamber, involving the participation of all MPs.

In the House of Lords, a parallel procedure is observed, where each bill is subjected to the collective scrutiny of all peers, analogous to the House of Commons' Committee of the Whole House. This inclusive approach in the Lords mirrors the comprehensive assessment seen in the Commons, ensuring a detailed examination of the bill in both houses.

(d) Report Stage. Following meticulous examination at the committee stage, the bill returns to the chamber for the report stage. This phase allows for the introduction and discussion of additional amendments.

However, it's customary in the House of Commons for the Speaker to refrain from selecting amendments for debate if they revisit topics previously deliberated upon in the process.

This stage primarily serves as a platform where all Members of Parliament can voice any remaining issues or considerations regarding the policy implications of the bill. It is an opportunity to ensure that any outstanding concerns are addressed and that the bill is refined before it progresses further in the legislative journey.

(e) **Third Reading.** The third reading serves as the concluding review of the bill within its originating house, typically conducted with brevity. At this juncture, Members of Parliament or Lords take one last look at the bill in its entirety before it crosses over to the other chamber to commence the legislative process anew.

Notably, in the House of Lords, this stage represents the final opportunity to propose and debate amendments, making it a critical point for peers to ensure the bill's provisions are as intended before it leaves their chamber.

(f) **Consideration of Amendments—'Ping Pong'.** As legislation advances through the parliamentary stages, it often undergoes modifications, at times significantly altering its original form. These adjustments necessitate careful examination in the originating House. Should these modifications find acceptance, the legislation progresses towards receiving the Monarch's formal consent.

Conversely, should there be disagreements, the originating House may either discard these amendments or propose alternate ones to the revising House. This initiatory House must then deliberate on whether to stand firm on its amendments, accept the proposed alternatives, seek a middle ground, or retract them entirely. This iterative dialogue, colloquially known as 'ping pong', continues until both Houses reach a consensus on the bill's final wording.

It is customary for the House of Lords, as the non-elected chamber, to eventually defer to the will of the elected House of Commons. Nonetheless, the Lords might persist with an amendment to prompt a thorough re-evaluation of the matter in the Commons.

(g) **Royal Assent.** Following successful navigation through both the House of Commons and the House of Lords, a bill's transformation into law hinges on receiving the Monarch's formal endorsement, known as the Royal Assent. This stage is largely ceremonial, as by long-standing constitutional tradition, the Royal Assent is invariably bestowed, rendering the bill an official Act of Parliament.

(h) **Specific Legislation for English Matters.** In an effort to address the absence of a distinct devolved body for England, a supplementary procedural step known as English Votes for English Laws has been instituted within the House of Commons. This step is applied to legislative proposals or certain sections thereof that exclusively pertain to England. Previously, there was a potential for laws applicable solely to England to be passed by the collective vote of the House of Commons, despite opposition from English MPs, due to support from representatives of Scotland, Wales, and Northern Ireland.

This procedural stage ensues after the Report Stage and before the Third Reading. At this juncture, the Speaker of the House identifies and certifies any clauses of a bill that are relevant only to England. Consequently, only those Members of Parliament who serve English constituencies are entitled to cast their vote on these matters. Should these MPs reject the specified provisions, the bill in question is returned for additional deliberation and potential amendment.

(i) **Authority of the House of Lords.** The House of Lords, although generally equipped with similar legislative powers as the House of Commons, often finds the legislative journey more arduous due to the usual absence of a government majority. The Lords possess the ability to impose amendments upon the government, and they can, in principle, reject a bill outright.

Nonetheless, their capacity to influence legislation is moderated by a blend of political conventions and statutory limitations, which underscore the principle that an unelected chamber should not indefinitely obstruct legislation approved by the democratically elected House of Commons.

This balance is encapsulated in the subsequent protocols, which delineate the extent of the Lords' legislative influence.

The Salisbury Convention:

Under this convention, the House of Lords typically accedes to the second reading of a government bill that enacts manifesto pledges of the elected ruling party. Despite this deference to the Commons at the initial stage, the Lords retain the prerogative to propose amendments during the bill's subsequent progression through Parliament.

Suspensory Veto Under the Parliament Acts 1911-1949:

The House of Lords' capacity to reject legislation is not absolute but rather suspensory. This means the Lords can only delay legislation, not permanently prevent it. If the Commons passes a bill which the Lords subsequently reject, and the Commons then passes it again in a new session, the legislation can proceed to the Monarch for Royal Assent without the Lords' concurrence. The critical temporal requirement for this process is that at least a year must have passed between the bill's second reading in the initial session and its third reading in the subsequent session.

Let's consider the hypothetical 'Climate Change Bill'. This bill, aimed at introducing stringent environmental regulations, was initially passed by the House of Commons.

However, it faces rejection in the House of Lords due to concerns about its impact on industries. The Commons, persistent in their environmental agenda, reintroduced the bill in the following parliamentary session. After a year has elapsed since its original Second Reading in the Commons, the bill is passed once more. Despite the Lords' continued resistance, the bill now moves forward to receive Royal Assent from the Monarch.

This sequence exemplifies how the House of Lords' veto is suspensory in nature under the Parliament Acts, demonstrating their limited capacity to indefinitely halt legislation.

2.4 Commencement

Following the granting of Royal Assent to legislation, its provisions typically do not become operative instantaneously. The norm is for the Act to encompass a stipulation that grants the government the discretion to instigate the law at a future point in time.

These provisions, known as commencement orders or regulations, fall under the umbrella of secondary legislation. Such orders specify which sections of the Act are to be activated (should it not be the entirety of the Act) and stipulate the commencement date. It's usual practice for different segments of an Act to be phased into legal force at varying times.

In the absence of any commencement directive within the legislation, the default position is that the law becomes effective upon receiving Royal Assent. Contemporary legislative practice typically ensures this immediate effect is explicitly articulated within the Act itself.

2.5 Modification, Revocation, and Expiry Provisions

Typically, legislation remains in force indefinitely, persisting as part of the statute book until Parliament decides otherwise. Parliament retains the authority to modify or entirely revoke any piece of legislation, effectively removing it from the corpus of active law.

Occasionally, a legislative act may incorporate a 'sunset provision', which dictates that certain sections or the entirety of the Act will lapse on a specified date. The primary benefit of this mechanism is that it compels Parliament to reassess the effectiveness and relevance of the legislation at a predetermined point in the future, ensuring its continued suitability and alignment with current needs and conditions.

3. Secondary Legislation

Secondary legislation, also known colloquially as delegated or subordinate legislation, statutory instruments, or simply regulations, encompasses various forms of legislation that derive their authority from primary legislation passed by Parliament.

This category of lawmaking allows the government to fill in more detailed or administrative content under the framework established by an Act of Parliament. Throughout this section, the term 'secondary legislation' will be consistently employed to describe these legal instruments.

Secondary legislation encompasses those legal rules and regulations formulated by government authorities under the empowerment of an Act of Parliament. It typically serves to enact detailed provisions essential for the practical implementation of governmental policies and administrative schemes.

This type of legislation ensures that complex or technical details, which are subject to change and may not be suitable for inclusion in the primary legislation, can be efficiently managed and updated as necessary.

3.1 How Secondary Legislation Is Created

Secondary legislation is brought into effect through two principal mechanisms:

(a) Negative Resolution Procedure. Under this procedure, the proposed secondary legislation is presented before both the House of Commons and the House of Lords. It becomes valid law on its specified commencement date unless a resolution to annul it is passed by either chamber within a statutory period, typically 40 days after presentation. Should no objection be registered within this timeframe, the legislation will be automatically enacted.

(b) Affirmative Resolution Procedure. Alternatively, secondary legislation can be implemented via the affirmative resolution procedure, which necessitates explicit approval from both Houses. The proposed legislation must be proactively supported through a formal vote in both the House of Commons and the House of Lords. Within the Commons, the legislation can be subject to debate either on the floor of the house or within a Delegated Legislation Committee. Neither House has the capacity to amend the proposed secondary legislation.

It is important to note that the procedures outlined in the Parliament Acts of 1911 and 1949 do not extend to secondary legislation, affording the House of Lords the authority to veto such legislation outright.

3.2 The Scope and Use of Henry VIII Clauses

Named after the Tudor monarch known for his assertive approach to governance, Henry VIII clauses grant the executive branch the authority to revise or repeal provisions within an Act of Parliament through secondary legislation. These powers typically facilitate minor, technical, or administrative adjustments to laws.

The employment of such powers is generally uncontroversial when applied to minor adjustments. However, broader applications that enable significant modifications to primary legislation have sparked debates concerning constitutional propriety. This is because they blur the traditional separation of powers, transferring substantial legislative functions from Parliament to government ministers.

The increasing reliance on Henry VIII clauses raises concerns about the balance of power between the legislature and the executive, and the potential erosion of parliamentary oversight and democracy.

3.3 Judicial Review of Secondary Legislation

Secondary legislation is established by the government under the authority delegated by an Act of Parliament, hence it is not directly crafted by the legislative body itself.

Consequently, it is susceptible to judicial scrutiny and can be invalidated by the courts if it is found to exceed the powers conferred by the primary legislation. This process, known as judicial review, is a mechanism that safeguards the rule of law by ensuring that the government's regulatory actions remain within the legal boundaries set by Parliament.

For instance, if a court determines that secondary legislation has been enacted outside the scope of its enabling statute or that it infringes upon fundamental principles of the rule of law, such legislation may be declared unlawful and thus void.

Additionally, when interpreting the scope of powers under which secondary legislation is made, courts may infer certain limitations to align the government's regulatory powers with the overarching principles of fairness and legality that underpin the rule of law.

4. Parliamentary Privilege and Freedom of Speech

Parliamentary privilege encompasses a collection of rights that safeguard the independence and functioning of Parliament, a cornerstone of which is the guarantee of uninhibited speech within its chambers.

This privilege is a manifestation of the separation of powers doctrine, affirming that the internal deliberations and expressions within Parliament are the preserve of the legislative body and not subject to external judicial scrutiny.

This special protection enables Members of Parliament (MPs) and Lords to engage in open and robust debate, secure in the knowledge that they are immune from litigation or legal repercussions for statements made in the course of parliamentary proceedings.

Additionally, it serves to reinforce the doctrine of parliamentary sovereignty by precluding judicial interference with the legislative process and the contents of the enacted laws.

4.1 The Sub Judicie Rule and Parliamentary Conduct

Parliamentary privilege comes with an implicit understanding that the privileges exercised will respect the judiciary and the legal processes in play. This mutual respect is embodied in the sub judicie rule, which instructs Members of Parliament and peers to refrain from discussing active legal cases within the confines of parliamentary debate.

The rationale for this restraint is the potential influence parliamentary discussions might exert on legal proceedings, thereby ensuring that judicial matters are determined solely within the judicial domain. Adherence to the sub judicie rule demonstrates Parliament's commitment to honouring the separation of powers by allowing the courts to operate without legislative encroachment or bias.

4.2 Exception to Privilege

While the doctrine of parliamentary privilege typically precludes the use of parliamentary discourse in judicial matters, there is a notable exception where the courts are permitted to consult the Hansard—the official transcript of debates in Parliament—as an interpretative aid for legislative intent.

This recourse is available under specific conditions: the legislation in question must present ambiguities; there must be an elucidatory statement by a minister within the debate; and such a statement must be clear enough to aid in the resolution of the ambiguity. This exception is an acknowledgment of the interconnectedness of legislative intent and judicial interpretation, providing a bridge where the legislative history may illuminate the path to understanding the law's purpose and scope.

Consider the case of a renewable energy company, EcoPower, which applied for subsidies under a new governmental renewable energy scheme. The scheme's enabling legislation was somewhat ambiguous about the eligibility criteria for these subsidies. EcoPower's application was initially rejected on the grounds that their technology didn't meet the criteria specified in the regulations.

However, during the parliamentary debate on the legislation, the responsible minister clearly stated that the subsidies were intended for a broad range of renewable technologies, including emerging and less conventional ones like EcoPower.

EcoPower challenged the rejection in court, arguing that their technology should be eligible for the subsidy based on the minister's statement. The court, acknowledging the ambiguity in the legislation, referred to the Hansard record of the parliamentary debate. Utilising the minister's explicit statement, the court interpreted the legislation to include a wider range of renewable technologies within the subsidy scheme, thus ruling in favour of EcoPower's eligibility.

This example illustrates how, in specific instances, the courts can draw on ministerial statements made during parliamentary debates to resolve ambiguities in legislation and to discern legislative intent.

CHAPTER 5. THE EVOLUTION OF MONARCHICAL POWER AND THE ROYAL PREROGATIVE

In the annals of British history, the Monarch was once the fountainhead of all executive, legislative, and judicial authorities, wielding absolute dominion. From the mediaeval period onwards, the Monarchy's direct rule was increasingly influenced by a cohort of advisors, culminating in a formalised Council.

By the 15th century, this evolved into the Privy Council, a body tasked with the day-to-day affairs of governance, subject to the Monarch's sanction during Council meetings. Advancing into the 18th century, the Monarch's advisors further coalesced into the Cabinet Council, a precursor to the modern-day Cabinet. Over time, the Monarch's direct involvement with this body dwindled, eventually ceasing altogether.

1. The 'Crown' as a Symbol of Government Structure

The historical narrative of governance in the UK underpins the present configuration of the central government. Even in contemporary times, the state's executive functions are performed under the auspices of the Crown. Ministers, embodying His/Her Majesty's Government, deliberate primarily in the Cabinet, although certain decisions are reserved for the Privy Council.

Hence, the Crown is not just the sovereign but symbolises the entire executive branch, encompassing the Monarch, Prime Minister, ministers, governmental departments, and the civil service, who collectively embody the government's operations.

This personification of the executive through the Crown has largely obviate the need to legally define the concept of the 'state' within the UK's constitutional framework.

1.1 The Monarch's Functions

In the United Kingdom, the Monarch holds the position of Head of State, symbolising the nation's unity and continuity, both domestically and on the international stage. The Monarch also serves as the Commander-in-Chief of the British Armed Forces, the Supreme Governor of the Church of England, and carries the title of Defender of the Faith.

Additionally, the Monarch oversees the administration of the self-governing Crown Dependencies, which include the Channel Islands and the Isle of Man, ensuring these territories' autonomy is respected while maintaining a constitutional link with the UK.

Furthermore, the British Monarch continues to be the Head of State for 15 other nations, commonly referred to as the Commonwealth realms. These nations chose to maintain the British Monarch as their ceremonial leader post-independence from the British Empire. Together, these countries, along with others that have historical ties to the Empire, constitute the Commonwealth, a political association presided over by the British Monarch.

This role reflects the UK's historical influence and the Monarch's symbolic authority across a diverse group of nations.

2. Range and Limits of the Royal Prerogative

Historically, the British Monarch wielded extensive powers as the ultimate authority across all state functions. These powers, known as the royal prerogative, are rooted in common law. With the ascendancy of parliamentary sovereignty, which has the power to nullify common law, a significant number of prerogative powers have been transferred to either the judiciary or Parliament, reflecting the modern separation of powers within the UK constitution.

Furthermore, many executive functions that were previously exercised under the royal prerogative are now authorised by Parliament through statutory provisions.

However, the royal prerogative has not been entirely dismantled. A core set of prerogative powers persists, and the interplay between these prerogative powers and statutory law can be intricate. Some of the remaining prerogative powers are significant in their constitutional impact and continue to play a role in the functioning of government.

These enduring powers of the royal prerogative and their interaction with enacted legislation form an essential aspect of contemporary UK constitutional law.

2.1 Governing Principles of Royal Prerogative Authority

(a) **Prohibition of New Prerogative Powers.** Following the establishment of parliamentary sovereignty with the Bill of Rights in 1688, it was enshrined that legislative power rests with Parliament, not the Crown. As a result, the government must look to Parliament to grant it any necessary authority rather than relying on the creation of new prerogative powers.

Thus, the scope of the royal prerogative is frozen as it stood before 1688; no new prerogative powers can emerge. To understand the current boundaries of royal prerogative, one must examine its historical scope and apply it to contemporary circumstances, acknowledging that its modern application is limited by the supremacy of statutory law.

Consider a scenario where the Foreign Secretary decides to establish a new type of diplomatic mission abroad, differing significantly from traditional embassies or consulates. The proposed mission would engage in cultural exchange and trade promotion rather than the usual diplomatic functions.

The decision to establish such a mission could be argued as falling under the royal prerogative relating to foreign affairs and the conduct of diplomacy.

Historically, the Crown has held the prerogative power to appoint diplomats and establish diplomatic missions. This power has been used over the years to adapt to changing international relations and diplomatic needs.

Therefore, even though the new diplomatic mission represents a modern adaptation, it could be seen as a lawful exercise of existing prerogative powers, rooted in the historical role of the Crown in managing foreign affairs. However, the creation of an entirely new type of diplomatic power or function, one that has no historical precedent or basis in the existing scope of royal prerogative, would require Parliamentary approval.

(b) Statutory Powers vs. Prerogative Powers. In instances where statutory provisions intersect with existing prerogative powers, the primary question becomes whether the prerogative or the statutory mandate should be exercised. When Parliament enacts legislation that encompasses areas previously under prerogative powers, it effectively supplants those powers with the new statutory authority.

Therefore, in cases of overlap, the enacted statute prevails, rendering the corresponding prerogative power subordinate or obsolete. This underlines the principle that statutory authority, reflecting the will of Parliament, takes precedence in the UK legal framework.

Imagine a scenario where Parliament passes a new Act that outlines specific procedures and conditions under which the UK military can be deployed overseas. Historically, the deployment of the armed forces is a prerogative power of the Crown, exercised by the government. However, this new Act sets out detailed criteria and requires parliamentary approval for certain types of military engagements.

In this situation, even though the government could argue that they are acting under the royal prerogative to deploy the military, the existence of the new Act means that its provisions must be followed. This is because the Act represents a more current and detailed expression of the legislative intent in the area of military deployment, thus overriding the more general and historical prerogative power.

Therefore, even if the government wanted to deploy forces in a manner consistent with historical prerogative practices, they would need to comply with the requirements of the new statute.

(c) **Prerogative Powers Cannot Oppose Parliamentary Intent.** The principle that statutory law supersedes prerogative powers extends to the notion that the Crown cannot employ prerogative powers to undermine or circumvent the intentions of Parliament. For example, when Parliament enacts a law but delegates the authority to the government to determine the timing of its implementation via commencement orders, the government is not at liberty to indefinitely postpone the law's activation in favour of existing prerogative powers. Such an action would effectively equate to an informal repeal of the Act using prerogative powers, which contravenes the overarching mandate that parliamentary intent must not be frustrated by the exercise of the Crown's prerogatives.

Suppose Parliament passes a comprehensive environmental protection act that sets out specific regulations and penalties for industries polluting rivers. The act empowers a government agency to enforce these regulations, but the government delays its implementation, preferring to use existing prerogative powers to negotiate voluntary agreements with industries for river protection.

In this scenario, the government's reliance on prerogative powers to form voluntary agreements, instead of implementing the parliamentary act, would be seen as an attempt to thwart the intention of Parliament. By not enforcing the specific regulations and penalties laid out in the act, the government would be neglecting the clear legislative directive and instead relying on a more informal and less stringent approach under prerogative powers.

This action could be challenged as unlawful, as it contravenes the express will of Parliament as manifested in the environmental protection act.

(d) Prerogative Powers Cannot Alter Legislation.
The royal prerogative is limited to the confines of

what is permitted by the law, and as such, it cannot be wielded to amend, modify, or override existing legislation or the established sources of UK law. The Crown's prerogative is therefore confined to the execution of existing legal provisions and does not extend to making alterations to the legal framework itself.

Imagine a situation where the government, using its prerogative powers, attempts to introduce a new public duty that requires all citizens to participate in a national cybersecurity program. This program would mandate citizens to install specific government-provided software on their personal devices for national security purposes.

In this scenario, the government's attempt to impose a new duty on citizens would effectively change the law, as it introduces a new obligation that was not previously legislated. Such a significant change in the legal obligations of citizens cannot be legitimately effected through prerogative powers but requires an Act of Parliament. The use of prerogative power in this manner would be challenging, as it oversteps the boundaries of what the prerogative can lawfully achieve and encroaches into the domain of legislative change, which is the purview of Parliament.

(e) **Statutory Provisions Do Not Apply to the Crown Without Explicit Stipulation.** According to a long-established interpretative principle, statutes are presumed not to bind the Crown unless they ex-

plicitly state otherwise or such an intention is un-
avoidably implied.

This principle acknowledges the unique constitutional
role of the Crown as the foundation of the central government. A notable instance of this principle is that the
Crown is exempt from taxation since it would be counter-
intuitive for Parliament to levy taxes on the very institution that executes governmental functions.

Consider a scenario where new environmental regulations are
introduced, requiring all industrial entities to adhere to strict
pollution control measures. These regulations, however, do
not explicitly mention government-owned enterprises. A government-run energy plant, part of the Crown's assets, continues to operate without conforming to these new environmental standards, arguing that the regulations do not apply
to it.

In this instance, unless the statute specifically states that
government entities are included or it can be necessarily implied, the Crown (represented by the government-run energy
plant) is not bound by these environmental regulations. This
situation illustrates the principle that the Crown enjoys a
unique status unless expressly or implicitly included in the
statute.

(f) Judicial Review of Prerogative Powers is In-
creasing

Historically, it was considered that certain prerogative actions, such as treaty negotiations, conferring honours, selecting a Prime Minister, or deploying military forces, were beyond judicial scrutiny, often due to their inherently political nature rather than legal. The courts traditionally refrained from adjudicating these matters to avoid overstepping into political territory.

However, contemporary judicial attitudes are evolving, with courts more readily examining the extent and exercise of prerogative powers. The judiciary has indicated that such powers may not be boundless and can be subject to constitutional constraints.

As a result, there is an increased tendency to review the application of prerogative powers, ensuring they do not exceed established legal and constitutional boundaries.

Consider a situation where the government uses its royal prerogative to withdraw from an international environmental treaty without any parliamentary approval or consultation. A group of environmental NGOs challenges this decision, arguing that it has significant implications for national policy and environmental protection.

The courts, acknowledging their expanded role in reviewing prerogative powers, agree to examine the case. They assess whether the government's use of the prerogative to unilaterally withdraw from the treaty falls within the legal bounds of such powers. In this case, the court could potentially rule that withdrawing from such a significant treaty, which has substantial policy implications and affects the nation's international obligations, exceeds the scope of prerogative powers and requires parliamentary scrutiny and approval.

This example illustrates the judiciary's increased readiness to scrutinise the exercise of prerogative powers, particularly when they have far-reaching effects.

3. Current Scope of Royal Prerogative

Today's royal prerogative powers are informally categorised into three types: 'ministerial', 'personal', and a range of miscellaneous or archaic prerogative powers.

3.1 The Exercise of Ministerial Prerogative Powers

Ministerial prerogative powers are those utilised by government ministers in the name of the Crown. Often, the Monarch's involvement is purely formal, endorsing decisions already taken by ministers.

In some cases, such as issuing passports, the Monarch's involvement is entirely absent, with the action being executed solely by the relevant government department under the direction of the minister. A key point of constitutional significance is that these powers, rooted in common law rather than explicit statutory authority, place the primary decision-making responsibility in the hands of ministers, with Parliament's role being more about oversight of these powers' application than their direct exercise. (The mechanisms through which Parliament exercises this oversight are examined subsequently.)

Key areas covered by ministerial prerogative powers include:

(a) **Sovereignty over territory**, including its acquisition or surrender.

(b) **Negotiation** and, subject to the Constitutional Reform and Governance Act 2010, **ratification** of international treaties.

(c) **General diplomatic conduct,** such as state recognition, diplomatic relations, and the appointment of envoys and High Commissioners (the latter term used for representatives in Commonwealth countries).

(d) **Deployment of military forces abroad**, including declarations of war.

(e) **Domestic use of armed forces** to uphold order in aid of civil authorities.

(f) **Appointment and dismissal** of ministers within the Prime Minister's cabinet.

(g) **Issuance and revocation of passports.**

(h) **Awarding pardons** and the ability to halt ongoing criminal prosecutions.

These ministerial prerogatives underscore the distinct separation between the executive's autonomy in certain areas of governance and the legislative oversight provided by Parliament.

3.2 Monarch's Discretionary Powers

Personal prerogative powers are those that the Monarch actively exercises in person. Although legally substantial, the Monarch's engagement with these powers is tightly regulated by established constitutional conventions, effectively circumscribing the Monarch's discretion.

These **personal prerogatives encompass:**

(a) **Selecting the Prime Minister;**

(b) **The authority to dissolve the government;**

(c) **The ability to prorogue Parliament,** effectively suspending its sessions; and

(d) **Conferring Royal Assent to bills**, thereby enacting them into law.

In practice, the exercise of these prerogatives is not a manifestation of the Monarch's personal will but rather a formal acknowledgement of the prevailing political conditions and the will of Parliament.

They serve as constitutional formalities that uphold the ceremonial aspect of the monarchy while ensuring the smooth functioning of parliamentary democracy.

3.3 Additional and Historical Prerogative Authorities

Beyond the aforementioned categories, there exists a collection of prerogative powers of a miscellaneous and often historical nature. These encompass a range of traditional rights and privileges that, while seldom invoked in contemporary times, remain part of the royal prerogatives.

They include the Crown's entitlement to mine for precious metals across the realm, the authority to oversee and sanction the construction of maritime harbours, the prerogative to issue coinage, and the somewhat ceremonial claim of the Crown to ownership of certain aquatic and avian species, notably sturgeons, dolphins, whales, and swans, which are found in particular sections of the River Thames.

These powers, while archaic, serve as reminders of the historical breadth of royal authority and its evolution into the constitutional monarchy of today.

3.4 Legislative and Judicial Prerogatives

While the bulk of the Monarch's historic legislative and judicial powers have been transferred to Parliament and the judiciary, a vestigial set of these powers endure as part of the royal prerogative.

(a) **Legislative Royal Prerogatives.** The Monarch's legislative prerogatives are now largely ceremonial or procedural. Orders in Council, a type of legislation, are promulgated by the Privy Council under the royal prerogative and receive formal approval during the Monarch's assent.

Additionally, the granting of Royal Assent, the final step for a bill to become law after parliamentary approval, remains a royal prerogative, symbolising the Crown's assent to legislative enactments.

(b) **Judicial Royal Prerogatives.** The remaining judicial prerogatives are typically exercised on behalf of the Crown by government ministers. These include the dispensation of pardons to convicted individuals and the cessation of ongoing prosecutions.

The Monarch's foundational role in the judicial system is symbolically retained in the Judicial Committee of the Privy Council, which adjudicates appeals from certain

Commonwealth countries. The Committee's rulings are technically presented as recommendations to the Monarch and are formally ratified at a meeting of the Privy Council.

4. Statutory Oversight of Royal Prerogative Powers

Rather than nullifying a royal prerogative power, Parliament may opt to legislate the manner in which such a power is wielded by introducing legal stipulations.

This statutory regulation ensures that the exercise of prerogative powers adheres to clearly defined legal parameters, thus maintaining a balance between the prerogative's inherent flexibility and the necessity for accountability and rule of law.

4.1 International Treaty Ratification

While the ratification of international treaties is a prerogative power, the Constitutional Reform and Governance Act 2010 mandates parliamentary oversight of this process.

(a) **Present Draft to Parliament for Twenty-One Days.** The government must present the draft text of any proposed international treaty to Parliament. Ratification can only proceed after a 21-day period during which neither the House of Commons nor the House of Lords has passed a resolution objecting to the ratification. This stipulation ensures that Parliament has the opportunity to scrutinise the terms of international treaties before they are ratified, reflecting a commitment to democratic oversight in the exercise of prerogative powers.

(b) **Subsequent Steps Following Parliamentary Rejection.** Should either chamber of Parliament vote against the ratification of a treaty, the government is entitled to present a case justifying its decision to proceed with ratification. Subsequently, the House of Commons is afforded an additional 21-day period to express its objection by passing a resolution against ratification. Absent such a resolution within this timeframe, the government is permitted to proceed with the ratification of the treaty. It is important to note that at this juncture, the House of Lords does not possess the authority to further impede the ratification process.

(c) **Exceptional Circumstances.** The government has the discretion to forgo the standard requirement of presenting a treaty to Parliament in situations deemed 'exceptional', although the criteria for what constitutes an exceptional case remain unspecified by legislation.

5. Oversight of Royal Prerogative Through Constitutional Conventions

Constitutional conventions play a pivotal role in the exercise of many prerogative powers, especially those directly exercised by the Monarch. To fully comprehend the operation of these powers, it's crucial to consider the established conventions alongside the formal legal stipulations.

Two key conventions are particularly noteworthy: the 'cardinal' convention, which pertains to the Monarch's interactions with Parliament, and the convention concerning the deployment of the armed forces abroad. Further discussion on the conventions governing other prerogative powers will be covered in subsequent sections.

5.1 The Cardinal Convention

The 'cardinal' convention underlines the principle that the Monarch invariably acts upon the counsel of her ministers, notably the Prime Minister. This convention highlights the ceremonial nature of the Monarch's role in affirming ministerial decisions.

The Monarch is entitled to three fundamental rights: consultation, encouragement, and cautioning the government. These rights are primarily exercised during the Monarch's weekly confidential meetings with the Prime Minister and are reinforced by the Monarch's access to government documents and communications with diplomatic envoys.

Despite any differences in opinion, it is paramount that the Monarch adheres to the ministers' advice, upholding her stance of political neutrality.

5.2 Authority in Military Deployment

The deployment of British armed forces in foreign territories remains a ministerial prerogative, indicating that the executive branch—specifically the government—has the authority to commit to military engagements without the need for parliamentary approval.

Yet, contemporary practices have evolved, particularly post-2003 following the Iraq conflict, to where the government now typically seeks the endorsement of the House of Commons prior to the initiation of military action abroad. This shift towards a more democratic process reflects the growing expectation for parliamentary debate and consensus on matters of national and international security.

6. Selecting the Prime Minister

Under the auspices of the royal prerogative, the Monarch is responsible for appointing the Prime Minister. However, this decision is directed by the constitutional convention which mandates that the Prime Minister should be a Member of Parliament (MP) who is capable of securing the confidence of the majority of the House of Commons.

Essentially, the Prime Minister should be in a position to maintain the support of more than half of the MPs, ensuring that they can effectively lead the government through the legislative body.

6.1 Commons Majority Support for Prime Minister

The enduring convention requiring the Prime Minister to maintain the backing of the majority of Members of Parliament typically leads to the Prime Minister being the leader of the political party that holds the majority of seats in the House of Commons.

(a) Post-General Election. Following a general election, it is possible for a different political party to secure the majority of seats within the House of Commons.

In such circumstances, the Prime Minister from the party that has lost its majority would traditionally resign. Subsequently, the leader of the new majority party would then be appointed as the new Prime Minister.

(b) Transition of Party Leadership. Outside of a general election cycle, a Prime Minister may decide to step down, typically by declaring their intention to relinquish both their role as the nation's leader and their position as the head of their political party. The party then orchestrates an internal leadership election, governed by its specific rules, to select a new leader.

Upon the election of a new leader, the departing Prime Minister tenders their resignation, and the Monarch proceeds to appoint the newly elected leader as the incoming Prime Minister.

(c) Scenarios of a Hung Parliament. A Hung Parliament arises when no single political party secures an outright majority after a general election. **In this situation:**

- The incumbent Prime Minister remains in their role until it becomes evident they no longer hold the confidence of the House of Commons;

- The Monarch remains neutral and refrains from intervening in the decision-making process regarding the appointment of the Prime Minister and the formation of the government;

- It is the responsibility of the political parties to ascertain who will lead the next government, which typically involves discussions and negotiations to forge potential coalitions or agreements among them; and

- Once a political agreement is solidified, signalling a clear route to command the confidence of the House of Commons, the current Prime Minister will step down if required, paving the way for the Monarch to appoint a successor who is able to command a majority in the Commons.

CHAPTER 6. CENTRAL GOVERNMENT OVERSIGHT AND RESPONSIBILITY

1. Government Structure and Leadership

Central government operates under the authority of the Crown, commonly referred to as 'His/Her Majesty's Government'. It is headed by the Prime Minister, who bears the overall responsibility for the administration of government. The Prime Minister is assisted by the Cabinet, composed of senior government ministers, typically Secretaries of State heading various government departments.

These Secretaries of State hold the overarching responsibility for the functioning and decisions of their respective departments. Supporting them are junior ministers, who take charge of specific sectors within the department. Permanent civil servants constitute the workforce of these departments, providing policy advice to ministers and executing the government's policies.

Accountability of the government and individual ministers to Parliament is upheld through the principle of ministerial responsibility, a doctrine that ensures ministers answer to Parliament for their departments' actions and their own conduct. This principle is vital for maintaining the checks and balances within the UK's political framework and is elaborated on later in this Chapter.

2. Role and Powers of the Prime Minister

The Prime Minister, formally designated as the First Lord of the Treasury, is acknowledged as the leader of Her Majesty's Government and holds overarching responsibility for the government's operations. The Prime Minister's accountability to Parliament is underpinned by the constitutional requirement that they must be a Member of Parliament, specifically the House of Commons.

While the Prime Minister's powers are not exhaustively enumerated in law, they encompass **a range of prerogatives shaped by historical conventions and practices**, including but not limited to:

(a) **Selecting and appointing members of the Cabinet and junior ministers**, thereby shaping the executive branch;

(b) **Setting the government's agenda,** including the legislative and policy priorities;

(c) **Representing the UK internationally,** including at summits and in negotiations with foreign leaders;

(d) **Overseeing the intelligence and security services** to ensure national security;

(e) **Deciding on the timing of general elections** within the limits set by law; and

(f) **Exercising influence over the Parliament's business** through control over the government's legislative program.

These powers, exercised through a combination of statutory authority and customary practice, underscore the Prime Minister's central role in guiding the direction and priorities of the UK government.

2.1 Structuring Government and Overseeing the Civil service

The Prime Minister wields considerable authority in shaping the structure of the central government. This includes the discretion to reorganise the government machinery by dissolving existing departments, consolidating multiple departments, or establishing new ones to better align with the government's objectives and respond to evolving priorities.

Alongside the organisational aspect, the Prime Minister bears overarching responsibility for the Civil Service.

This encompasses the appointment of high-ranking civil servants who play pivotal roles in the functioning of government departments.

Moreover, the Prime Minister is involved in key public sector appointments, ensuring that leadership positions are filled by individuals who can effectively implement the government's policies and uphold the principles of public service. These responsibilities underscore the Prime Minister's integral role in the stewardship of the government's administrative apparatus.

2.2 Prime Minister's Constitutional Functions

The Prime Minister serves as the principal constitutional advisor to the Monarch, fulfilling a pivotal role in maintaining the relationship between the Crown and the government. This entails regular weekly audiences with the Monarch and, on occasion, consultations with the Heir Apparent, the Prince of Wales.

Furthermore, the Prime Minister oversees the interaction between the central UK government and the devolved administrations of Scotland, Wales, and Northern Ireland, ensuring cohesive governance across the different tiers of government within the United Kingdom.

The Prime Minister also holds the prerogative to propose the dissolution of Parliament and the calling of an early general election. This request is presented to the House of Commons, and an election is triggered if it secures the approval of at least two-thirds of the total number of Members of Parliament, showcasing the Prime Minister's significant influence over the parliamentary cycle.

2.3 Oversight of National security and Intelligence

The Prime Minister is charged with the overarching responsibility for the nation's security and intelligence affairs. This role encompasses the appointment of the chiefs of the intelligence services—including MI5, which handles domestic security; MI6, which oversees foreign intelligence; and GCHQ, which is responsible for signals intelligence and cybersecurity.

Furthermore, the Prime Minister supervises the development and implementation of counter-terrorism strategies, ensuring that national security is upheld through coordinated intelligence efforts and policies.

2.4 Armed Forces

The Prime Minister holds the ultimate decision-making authority regarding the deployment of the UK's armed forces. While this power is contingent upon obtaining consent from the House of Commons, the Prime Minister directs military engagements beyond national borders as well as the utilisation of military resources to aid civil authorities in maintaining public order domestically. This role underscores the Prime Minister's pivotal position in matters of national defence and public safety.

2.5 Diplomacy and International Negotiations

The Prime Minister serves as the nation's foremost representative at key global forums such as NATO, and the G7 summit. Additionally, the Prime Minister was charged with spearheading the complex negotiations that orchestrated the United Kingdom's departure from the European Union, underscoring the role's central importance in diplomatic affairs and international strategy.

3. Formation of the Ministerial Cabinet

Upon their appointment by the Monarch, the Prime Minister is tasked with assembling a government, necessitating the selection of ministers to head the various departments that constitute the central government.

While these ministerial appointments are formally enacted by the Monarch based on the Prime Minister's recommendations, in practice, it is the Prime Minister who wields the decisive authority in these selections. The senior-most ministers comprise the Cabinet, whereas all other ministers are considered junior. The Prime Minister's selection process is subject to a number of limitations and considerations.

3.1 Parliamentary Seat Requirement for Ministers

Traditionally, ministers are required to hold a seat in either the House of Commons or the House of Lords, a practice which ensures government accountability to Parliament. The majority of ministers are Members of Parliament (MPs), highlighting the preeminence of the

House of Commons within the parliamentary frame-work.

In some instances, individuals appointed as ministers may not initially hold a parliamentary seat; these individuals are typically conferred a life peerage and subsequently inducted into the House of Lords soon after their ministerial appointment.

3.2 Constraints of Political Dynamics on the Prime Minister

Political considerations significantly curtail the autonomy of the Prime Minister in selecting ministers. The enduring tenure of a Prime Minister hinges on maintaining the support of their political party, particularly its parliamentary members.

Consequently, Prime Ministers must continually cultivate and confirm backing from their fellow Members of Parliament, effectively subjecting them to a degree of indirect regulation by their party apparatus.

4. The Cabinet

4.1 Cabinet Structure

The Cabinet, the UK government's principal decision-making body, is composed of the Prime Minister and the most senior ministers.

Members typically include:

(a) **The Prime Minister**, who chairs the Cabinet;

(b) **The Chancellor of the Exchequer**, responsible for the nation's finances;

(c) **The Chief Secretary to the Treasury**, serving as the Chancellor's deputy;

(d) **Secretaries of State** heading various government departments;

(e) **The Lord Chancellor**, who is also the Secretary of State for Justice;

(f) **The Leader of the House of Commons,** tasked with managing government business in the Commons;

(g) **The Leader of the House of Lords,** similarly responsible for government business in the Lords;

(h) **The Chief Whip**, charged with ensuring party members in Parliament vote in line with government policies.

4.2 Cabinet Functions

The Cabinet holds the central executive authority in the UK government, tasked with deciding on government policy and strategy. The Cabinet typically convenes weekly, where ministers deliberate on major policy issues.

Key decisions expected to be addressed by the Cabinet encompass:

(a) **Engaging in military initiatives or operations;**

(b) **Shaping the government's legislative priorities,** annually presented in the Queen's Speech;

(c) **Handling constitutional matters**, including the monarchy, parliamentary reforms, and alterations to the devolution arrangements with Scotland, Wales, and Northern Ireland;

(d) **Major domestic policy issues;**

(e) **Significant international and European Union affairs;**

(f) **Management of national crises**, such as terrorism, and other urgent security matters.

4.3 Substructure of the Cabinet: Cabinet Committees

Alongside the primary Cabinet body, there exist subsidiary groups known as Cabinet committees. These subgroups are constituted by the Prime Minister, who also selects their members, typically comprising a mix of Cabinet ministers and junior ministers.

These committees serve as platforms for detailed examination and discussion of specific issues, enabling decisions to be made without convening a full Cabinet meeting. Resolutions passed within Cabinet committees carry the same weight and authority as those made by the full Cabinet.

4.4 Principle of Collective Responsibility and Confidentiality

The principle of collective responsibility ensures that deliberations within the Cabinet and its subcommittees remain strictly confidential, fostering an environment conducive to frank and open dialogue among ministers. Upon reaching a consensus, all ministers are expected to publicly support and adhere to the decision, regardless of personal viewpoints.

4.5 Evolving Practices in Government Decision-Making

The evolving landscape of governance, marked by its complexity and immediacy, has rendered the traditional weekly Cabinet meeting insufficient for addressing the multifaceted challenges faced by modern governments.

In response, a trend has emerged where Prime Ministers often bypass the broader Cabinet framework, opting instead for consultation with a select cohort of ministers and personal advisors. Subsequently, the Cabinet is apprised of the resolutions already determined through these more intimate consultations.

5. Structure of Government Departments

The UK government's framework comprises approximately 25 distinct departments, each charged with the formulation and execution of policies within their specialised domains.

A snapshot of these departments includes:

(a) **The Department for Education**, focused on educational policies and systems;

(b) **The Ministry of Defence,** overseeing national defence strategies and military operations;

(c) **HM Treasury,** responsible for economic, fiscal, and financial matters;

(d) **The Department for Transport**, managing transportation policies and infrastructure; and

(e) **The Foreign & Commonwealth Office**, handling the UK's diplomatic affairs and international relationships.

5.1 Ministerial Leadership

At the helm of each governmental department stands a Secretary of State, tasked with the overarching supervision and accountability of the department's operations to Parliament. Supporting the Secretary are various junior ministers, each overseeing specific segments within the department's purview.

The ministerial hierarchy beneath the Secretary of State is tiered, with a Minister of State assuming a higher rank than a Parliamentary Under Secretary of State, reflecting the gradations of responsibility and authority within the departmental structure.

5.2 Law and Policy Governance

Government departments diligently execute their duties in line with established laws and policies. The legal framework that underpins a department's functions may originate from the royal prerogative or be enshrined in statutory provisions.

Legislative enactments often delegate specific powers to Secretaries of State; theoretically, these powers are vested in any Secretary of State but, practically, are exercised by the one overseeing the pertinent area of governance.

The Carltona Principle:

The Carltona Principle is an accepted convention which asserts that powers assigned to a Secretary of State by an Act of Parliament are implicitly understood to be exercisable by appropriate civil servants within the minister's department. This principle acknowledges that the practical realities of governance necessitate delegation within departments.

Consider the scenario where the Secretary of State for the Home Department holds the power to issue or refuse passports under an Act of Parliament. Given the large volume of passport applications and decisions, it is impractical for the Secretary of State to personally handle each case.

Under the Carltona Doctrine, this responsibility is delegated to civil servants within the Home Office, who make decisions on passport applications on behalf of the Secretary of State. This delegation is understood to be within the scope of the original power granted by Parliament to the Secretary of State, ensuring that the process remains efficient while still adhering to the legal framework established by Parliament.

5.3 Policy Formulation

Government departments are also tasked with crafting new policy directives, frequently inspired by the governing party's manifesto commitments set forth during electoral campaigning. The electoral success of the party is perceived as a mandate to implement these policies. If legislative amendments are required for the policy's execution, the government will propose a bill in Parliament to secure the legal modifications needed for policy implementation.

5.4 The Civil Service Backbone

The Civil Service comprises individuals employed within government departments, with their **responsibilities encompassing:**

(a) **Processing** decisions in line with established laws and governmental directives, such as managing passport applications or welfare claims.

(b) **Providing** support to ministers in the ideation and refinement of policy measures.

(c) **Enacting** and administering newly introduced policies.

Civil servants are officially considered servants of the Crown, pledging their service to the institution of the monarchy rather than to individual government ministers.

Their roles are enduring, transcending the tenure of any particular political party in power, which necessitates an adherence to political neutrality. They are expected to offer unbiased advice to ministers, who then make informed policy decisions, followed by the civil servants' neutral implementation of these policies.

6. The Privy Council

The Privy Council is a historical body that precedes the current Cabinet in origin. Although its significance has been largely eclipsed by the Cabinet's ascendancy, the Privy Council continues to play a ceremonial role in the governance structure. Its primary function in the modern context is to formally endorse decisions that have been deliberated and concluded in other governmental forums.

6.1 Privy Council Duties

The Privy Council primarily enacts Orders in Council, which stand as a distinctive category of legal instruments. A subset of these orders emanates directly from the royal prerogative, granting them the status of primary legislation, albeit less commonly utilised in contemporary governance. The majority of Orders in Council, however, are promulgated under the authority vested in the Privy Council by Acts of Parliament, thus constituting a form of delegated or secondary legislation.

Additionally, the Privy Council wields the prerogative authority to validate the language of Royal Charters, thereby instituting new public entities, academic bodies, and professional associations.

6.2 Appointments

Membership to the Privy Council is conferred for life and is granted by the Monarch, acting on the recommendations of the Prime Minister. Conventionally, all members of the Cabinet are bestowed with this appointment.

6.3 Privy Council Assemblies

The Privy Council's assemblies are conducted in a confidential manner, typically with the Monarch's participation. The Monarch is generally accompanied by a select group of Privy Councillors, all of whom are serving government ministers.

6.4 The Judicial Committee

The Judicial Committee of the Privy Council (JCPC) plays a significant legal role, adjudicating on legal disputes from Commonwealth countries or British Overseas Territories that do not possess their own ultimate appellate court. Such jurisdictions availing themselves of the JCPC's services include various Caribbean nations like the Bahamas and Jamaica, as well as British Overseas Territories such as the Falkland Islands and the Cayman

Islands. The hearings are conducted by appointed members of the Supreme Court who also serve as Privy Councillors, ensuring the delivery of judicial functions.

7. Ministerial Responsibility and the Imperative of Accountability

The government's legitimacy hinges on maintaining the trust and support of the House of Commons, with 'support' signifying a backing for governmental actions.

As government officials are drawn from the membership of both the House of Commons and the House of Lords, they are obliged to justify and explain the government's conduct. This duty encompasses engaging in parliamentary debates, responding to enquiries, and facilitating parliamentary committees' scrutiny.

This section will first explore the dimensions of accountability and subsequently delve into the parliamentary mechanisms that empower MPs and Lords to scrutinise and hold ministers answerable.

7.1 Collective Responsibility

Collective ministerial responsibility mandates that all government ministers must publicly uphold and defend the policies of the government in Parliament. This doctrine is founded on two principal components: confidentiality and unanimity.

(a) **Confidentiality.** The formulation of governmental policy is conducted under the seal of confidentiality. This enables ministers to candidly exchange views within the confines of privacy, assured that their deliberations will not be disclosed externally, whether to the public domain or to Parliament.

(b) **Unanimity.** Upon the government's conclusion on a policy, typically reached through Cabinet consensus, it is incumbent upon all ministers to uphold that policy publicly and in parliamentary discussions. Should a minister find themselves unable to support a specific government policy, it is incumbent upon them to relinquish their ministerial position.

Imagine a situation where the Cabinet, after extensive deliberations, decides to engage in a military intervention overseas.

The Minister of Defence, despite initially supporting alternative strategies, is bound by the principle of unanimity to endorse this decision publicly.

However, after considering the implications and potential consequences of the intervention, the Minister of Defence finds themselves in fundamental disagreement with the Cabinet's decision. Confronted with a situation where they cannot publicly support the decision without compromising their own beliefs, the Minister of Defence chooses to resign from their position.

This resignation reflects the adherence to the principle of unanimity, where maintaining a united front on government policies is paramount, even at the cost of losing a Cabinet member.

(c) **Exceptions to Collective Responsibility.** On rare occasions, the Prime Minister may choose to waive the principle of collective responsibility, usually in the context of referendums, to permit ministers to publicly advocate different stances on the issue at hand. This has historically occurred thrice since 1945, enabling ministers to partake in referendum campaigns that align with their personal convictions, notwithstanding the collective stance of the government.

As the debate over the UK's continued membership in the European Union grew more intense, Prime Minister Cameron announced the referendum on EU membership, acknowledging the wide range of opinions on this matter within his Cabinet. To maintain cabinet unity and respect the differing views on this critical issue, he suspended the usual rules of collective responsibility.

This unprecedented move allowed members of the Cabinet, including high-profile figures like Boris Johnson and Michael Gove, to openly campaign for the 'Leave' side, while others, including the Prime Minister himself, campaigned for 'Remain'.

This suspension of collective responsibility was essential in allowing ministers to freely express their views and campaign according to their beliefs on this momentous national decision.

7.2 Individual Responsibility

Ministers hold personal accountability for their conduct and the functioning of their respective departments. They are obliged to provide explanations and justifications for their department's operations and their own actions.

(a) **Obligation of Truthfulness to Parliament.** Central to the concept of ministerial accountability is the obligation for ministers not to deceive Parliament. Effective parliamentary scrutiny is predicated on the accuracy and reliability of the information provided by ministers. Should a minister inadvertently provide incorrect information to Parliament, they are expected to rectify such errors at the earliest opportunity. Deliberate deception of Parliament by a minister necessitates their resignation.

(b) **Ministerial Accountability and Responsibility in Departmental Affairs:**

• **Obligation to Provide Explanations:** Ministers are duty-bound to explain their departmental actions to Parliament. This entails addressing queries and issues raised by members of Parliament, thereby channelling public inquiries and apprehensions through elected officials. Ministers are expected to engage with these issues in a way that assures Parliament of their competence and the integrity of the government's operations.

• **Assumption of Responsibility:** Ministers have the obligation to assume responsibility for their department's conduct, particularly in instances where they themselves are culpable. This means they are expected to address and respond to Parliamentary critiques in a satisfactory manner, ensuring that Parliament retains confidence in their capability to govern effectively. In extreme circumstances, this could involve the minister's resignation from their post.

- **Distinguishing the Two.** There is a recognised distinction between policy failures, for which the minister is accountable, and operational issues, for which the minister must provide explanations. In cases of policy failure, the minister is expected to accept responsibility for any shortcomings and to address the consequences. For operational issues, the minister is responsible for reporting to Parliament, outlining what went wrong, and taking appropriate measures to prevent future failures.

(c) **Standards of Ministerial Conduct.** Ministers are expected to maintain the utmost standards of personal conduct, abiding by both the ethical guidelines and the expectations of their public roles. The Ministerial Code serves as the benchmark for these standards, setting out the ethical framework within which ministers must operate.

It emphasises the avoidance of any conflicts between public duties and private interests. While personal conduct may not always directly contravene specific provisions within the Code, ministers can still face resignation if their actions result in substantial public controversy or embarrassment to the government.

In such cases, it is the Prime Minister who ultimately determines the appropriateness of a minister's conduct and whether it warrants resignation.

7.3 Parliamentary Accountability

The principle that the government must retain the confidence of the House of Commons underscores the need for robust parliamentary scrutiny. The House of Commons employs several mechanisms to hold the government accountable, with parallel processes in the House of Lords for its members.

(a) **Prime Minister's Question Time (PMQs).** PMQs is a weekly session where the Prime Minister stands before MPs to answer questions regarding the government's policies and decisions. This session is a platform for the Leader of the Opposition to pose six questions to the Prime Minister, often sparking a lively exchange.

(b) **Ministerial Questions.** Daily sessions are held where Members of Parliament can pose inquiries to ministers representing various government departments. These departments are scheduled on a rotational basis, typically facing Parliamentary questioning every five weeks. Enquiries must pertain to the department's remit and exclude topics such as local authority issues, the Monarchy, foreign state affairs, devolved matters in Northern Ireland, Scotland, or Wales, and ongoing legal cases.

MPs can submit written questions at any point, with the expectation that the concerned department will deliver a response within a seven-day period.

(c) Allocation for Opposition. Out of the parliamentary schedule, 20 days are reserved for opposition parties to raise debates on subjects of their choosing, to which the government must provide a counter-argument or clarification.

(d) Urgent Questions. MPs can request the Speaker's permission to raise immediate issues for discussion. If the Speaker concurs on the urgency and public significance of the topic, a minister is summoned to answer promptly.

(e) Select Committees. Select Committees are specialised groups tasked with in-depth government oversight. Departmental Select Committees focus on individual government departments, while others have a broader scope.

These committees conduct investigations, interrogate ministers and experts, and publish reports that demand a government response. Occasionally, these reports are brought to the chamber floor for debate.

Liaison Committee:

Comprising Select Committee chairs, the Liaison Committee convenes biannually to engage the Prime Minister in comprehensive dialogue, extending beyond the scope of PMQs.

CHAPTER 7. DEVOLU-
TION

Devolved governance represents the distribution of powers from a sovereign, central authority to subsidiary, regional entities. Within the United Kingdom, composed of the four distinct nations of England, Scotland, Wales, and Northern Ireland, the legislative framework has facilitated the devolution of powers to Scotland, Wales, and Northern Ireland.

This devolutionary framework establishes distinct legislative bodies and administrations for these nations, empowering them to legislate autonomously in designated areas of policy and governance.

1. The Legal Framework of Devolution

1.1 Establishment of 'Permanence' in Scotland and Wales

The legislative framework of the United Kingdom has affirmed the enduring status of the Scottish Parliament and Government, as well as the Welsh Parliament and Government, as integral components of the nation's constitutional structure.

This legal acknowledgment underscores their permanence, ensuring that these devolved entities cannot be dissolved without the express consent of the Scottish or Welsh populace, ascertained through a referendum.

1.2 Distinct Status of Devolution in Northern Ireland

The devolutionary arrangement for Northern Ireland is distinct from that of Scotland and Wales, having been established through the Belfast Agreement in 1998, commonly known as the Good Friday Agreement.

This landmark accord involved not only an international treaty between the United Kingdom and the Republic of Ireland but also encompassed a comprehensive pact among the political parties of Northern Ireland.

The Good Friday Agreement paved the way for the establishment of the Northern Ireland Assembly and the Northern Ireland Executive to administer the region. The unique aspect of this agreement is its provision for a referendum to gauge public opinion on the potential unification with the Republic of Ireland.

Should there be indications of a majority preference in Northern Ireland for unification, a plebiscite will be organised to allow the populace to decide between remaining a constituent of the UK or joining the Republic of Ireland.

2. Application of the Sewel Convention

The Sewel Convention is a political agreement that acknowledges the legislative autonomy of Scotland, Wales, and Northern Ireland by stipulating that the UK Parliament will not normally legislate on devolved matters without the consent of the devolved legislatures.

This convention operates through the mechanism of 'legislative consent motions' where the devolved bodies signal their agreement or disagreement to the UK Parliament's proposed legislation on devolved issues.

It is crucial to note that while the convention is a matter of constitutional respect, it is not legally binding. The use of the term 'normally' signifies that the UK Parliament retains the ultimate legal authority to legislate on any matter, including those within the purview of devolved administrations.

Therefore, even in instances where consent from a devolved institution is withheld, the UK Parliament maintains the legal capacity to enact the proposed legislation.

3. Judicial Oversight of Devolved Legislation and Constraints on Legislative Authority

The legislative output of the devolved parliaments in Scotland, Wales, and Northern Ireland is subject to judicial review to ensure it falls within their designated competencies. If these bodies enact legislation that oversteps their powers, the judiciary holds the authority to invalidate such legislation. The judiciary in the respective nations can defer to the UK Supreme Court for final adjudication.

Circumstances that could trigger judicial intervention include instances where devolved legislation:

(a) **Encroaches upon areas** not devolved to them, thereby exceeding their legislative remit; or

(b) **Contravenes the provisions** of the European Convention on Human Rights (ECHR).

It's important to note that while the UK was a member of the European Union, the devolved governments were additionally restrained from passing legislation that conflicted with EU law. Following the UK's departure from the EU, these limitations have been lifted. The devolved bodies now possess the capacity to legislate in divergence from EU law and to adapt retained EU law within the scope of their legislative authority.

Nevertheless, this ability is regulated by the UK government's delineation of specific domains of retained EU law that are beyond the amending reach of the devolved legislatures.

4. Referral to the Supreme Court for Devolved Legislation

Prior to a bill receives Royal Assent within a devolved legislature, there exists a provision for it to be referred to the UK Supreme Court.

This referral process is a safeguard to ascertain whether the proposed legislation is within the jurisdictional legislative competence of the devolved body. The referral seeks to preempt any potential legal challenges post-enactment by resolving questions of legislative competence in advance.

The Supreme Court, therefore, acts as a preemptive check on the authority of devolved legislatures, ensuring that the legislation they pass is within their legal boundaries as defined by devolution law.

CHAPTER 8. JUDICIAL OVERSIGHT

1. Definition of Judicial Oversight

Judicial review serves as the primary mechanism through which the judiciary oversees the legality of decisions or actions undertaken by executive authorities. It is a process whereby the courts examine the processes and legalities underpinning executive decisions, rather than appraising the substantive merits of the outcomes themselves.

This function underscores a key aspect of the rule of law, ensuring that public bodies exercise their powers within the legal framework and do not overstep the boundaries set by legislation or the common law. Judicial review thereby upholds the principle that governance must be conducted within the confines of legality, and it empowers courts to hold the executive accountable for its adherence to legal norms.

Key Considerations in Judicial Review:

In the realm of judicial review, three pivotal considerations determine the trajectory and outcome of an application. These are scrutinised in depth as follows:

(a) **Admissibility of the Application:** The initial concern lies in ascertaining whether the application for judicial review fulfils the criteria set forth for a viable claim. This encompasses a range of preliminary checks, such as the timeliness of the application, the standing of the applicant, and the exhaustion of alternative remedies.

(b) **Establishment of Grounds for Review:** The second concern addresses the substantive legal basis of the application. The applicant must demonstrate that one or more established grounds for judicial review are met. These grounds typically include illegality, irrationality, procedural impropriety, and proportionality. Each ground represents a different way in which the decision-making process of a public body may have fallen foul of legal standards.

(c) **Appropriate Remedies:** The final concern is the determination of a suitable remedy should the judicial review succeed. Remedies in judicial review can range from quashing the original decision, mandating a particular action, prohibiting an action from being taken, to merely declaring the rights of the parties involved. The choice of remedy is guided by the courts' discretion, the nature of the legal breach, and the practicalities of the situation.

Collectively, these considerations form the bedrock upon which the judicial review process is built, ensuring that it serves as an effective tool for the maintenance of legal accountability by public authorities.

2. Prerequisites for Judicial Oversight

2.1 Conditions for Applying for Judicial Review

For an application for judicial review to proceed, it must be directed towards an entity with public authority.

The scope of what constitutes a public body encompasses:

(a) **Governmental Entities:** This category includes central government figures like Secretaries of State and various governmental departments, which are the archetypal subjects of judicial review due to their public decision-making roles.

(b) **Local Authorities:** Entities at the municipal or local level, such as city or county councils, fall within the purview of judicial review as their actions often impact public rights and interests.

(c) **Statutory and Prerogative Agencies:** Bodies that have been established by legislative statutes or under the royal prerogative, which are endowed with public functions, can also be scrutinised through judicial review.

Conversely, the judicial review mechanism is not applicable to private sector entities such as businesses, non-governmental organisations, and charities, unless they are executing roles or functions on behalf of the state that affect public rights. This distinction ensures that judicial review remains a tool for regulating public, not private, power.

2.2 Presence of a Contract

The existence of a contractual agreement between a public body and a private entity typically necessitates the resolution of disputes within the domain of private law, as opposed to public law through judicial review.

Consider a scenario where a National Health Service (NHS) trust enters into an agreement with a medical supplies company to provide hospital equipment. If the NHS trust withholds payment, claiming the equipment is substandard, the supplier contends the equipment meets the agreed specifications.

The resolution of this disagreement would be pursued through the courts by way of a contract law claim, not through judicial review, as it pertains to the enforcement of a private commercial agreement.

2.3 Adherence to Proper Procedures

For a claim of judicial review to be considered, it must be initiated and progressed following the prescribed legal procedures.

(a) Pre-Action Protocol for Judicial Review

Before commencing formal judicial review proceedings, claimants are expected to adhere to the pre-action protocol for judicial review.

This involves sending a detailed pre-action letter to the prospective defendant, outlining the claim's basis and the issues at hand. The defendant is typically given 14 days to provide a substantial reply.

This step encourages parties to settle disputes without resorting to court and, if litigation is unavoidable, ensures that the parties are clear about each other's positions.

(b) Permission Stage

Judicial review is a two-stage process. The initial stage involves seeking permission from the court to pursue a judicial review claim. The claimant must submit an application, which is usually assessed based on the documents provided, including the defendant's written response. Sometimes, the presiding judge may decide to hold a preliminary hearing to resolve complex issues.

If permission is denied, the claim cannot progress further. If permission is granted, the case advances to the second stage, which involves a comprehensive court hearing where the substantive issues are thoroughly examined.

2.4 Impact on Claimant's Situation

A judicial review may be refused at the permission stage if the court deems that the outcome would not materially differ for the applicant, regardless of the claim's success.

Consider a university that has a formal appeals process for students who wish to contest their exam results.

Jack submits an appeal regarding his final thesis grade, but due to a procedural oversight, the university fails to consider his appeal within the stipulated time frame. The university later reviews Jack's thesis, adhering to the proper process, and upholds the original grade, having taken into account all the relevant academic criteria. If Jack were to seek judicial review of the initial procedural error, the court might determine that a successful review would not affect the final decision concerning his grade.

Therefore, it may refuse the judicial review on the basis that the outcome for Jack would not be substantially altered.

2.5 Adherence to Time Constraints

For a judicial review to be admissible, the claim should be initiated without undue delay and, under no circumstances, should it exceed three months from the incident's occurrence.

This period usually starts from the date the decision in question is communicated to the claimant. The court retains the discretion to reject a claim for judicial review within the three-month window if it deems that the claimant has not acted with sufficient expediency.

In instances where the judicial review pertains to a planning resolution, the claim must be filed within a more stringent time frame of six weeks following the decision's announcement.

2.6 Exclusivity of Procedure for Public Law Matters

The avenue of judicial review is reserved exclusively for disputes under public law. This principle, known as procedural exclusivity, stipulates that grievances against public bodies must be addressed through judicial review rather than ordinary civil litigation processes.

(a) **Cases Involving Public and Private Law Components.** In certain situations, when a case encompasses both public and private law elements, it may be adjudicated through the standard civil litigation route.

Consider a situation where a local council has engaged a contractor to refurbish community centres. The contract stipulates specific renovation standards and deadlines. Suppose the council withholds payment, claiming the work does not meet the contractually agreed standards, despite the contractor asserting completion as per the specifications.

Here, while the council's decision implicates public law due to its status as a public body, the contractual relationship permits the dispute to be settled within the remit of private law. Hence, the contractor could pursue a breach of contract claim in the civil courts instead of seeking judicial review.

2.7 Review ability of the Issues Presented

For a matter to be subject to judicial review, the issues at stake must fall within the purview of matters that the courts are equipped and willing to evaluate.

The courts typically refrain from considering hypothetical queries or speculative scenarios; they require an active, current dispute in which the parties seeking review have a direct and substantial interest.

A local education authority announces a future policy to re-structure the funding for after-school programs, which may potentially reduce the availability of certain services. A local parents' group, anticipating negative effects from this policy, seeks to challenge the decision before it is implemented.

However, since the changes have not yet taken effect and the actual impact is not yet ascertainable, the courts might view the case as premature and decline to review it. The group would likely need to wait until the policy is operational and its effects are felt before their concerns become justi-ciable in a judicial review.

2.8 Fact-based Disputes

Judicial review is designed to assess the legality of decisions made by public bodies, not to adjudicate on disputes that hinge on factual determinations.

As such, cases that primarily involve issues of fact rather than questions of law are better suited to resolution within the traditional court system.

A patient is denied specialised treatment by a healthcare trust, which claims the treatment is not clinically indicated for the patient's condition. The patient believes this decision is based on an incorrect assessment of their medical records.

Seeking judicial review to challenge this decision would be inappropriate since the crux of the dispute involves the accuracy of the medical judgement—a matter of fact rather than a legal error. Instead, this case should be pursued through the normal litigation process, where a court or tribunal could examine the medical evidence in detail.

2.9 Standing Requirements for Judicial Review

For an entity to initiate a judicial review, it must demonstrate a significant connection to the issue at hand, known

as legal standing. The courts evaluate standing at the preliminary permission phase, denying claims where the applicant's interest is not sufficiently direct or vested.

A coalition of environmental organisations seeks to contest a
government decision to approve a large-scale industrial project in a protected area. Although no single member of the
coalition may have been directly affected by the decision, the
coalition collectively represents the environmental interests
that the project could impact. The court might consider the
coalition's established advocacy and stewardship over environmental matters as indicative of its standing to bring the
case.

Note: In instances where standing is not self-evident, the
court may defer the assessment until the full hearing to allow
a comprehensive evaluation of the legal and factual contexts.

(a) **Collective Action by Associations.** Ordinarily,
individual parties lacking the standing to sue cannot
gain it by simply forming a group. Nevertheless,
courts have begun recognising that organisations,
particularly those with a track record of advocacy
and no clear alternative litigant, may possess the re-
quisite interest to proceed.

An educational trust, dedicated to upholding academic integrity, wishes to challenge a university's admission policies that allegedly dilute academic standards. Despite no individual member being directly affected, the trust's dedication to educational standards and its lack of a clear alternative litigant could provide it with the standing necessary to pursue judicial review.

2.10 Judicial Oversight as a Last Resort

Judicial review is intended to be utilised only after all other remedial avenues have been pursued and found inadequate. Specifically, if there is an established tribunal or alternative legal mechanism capable of reviewing the public body's decision, these should be employed prior to seeking judicial review.

A healthcare professional faces disciplinary action from a regulatory body, which has the potential to result in the loss of their medical licence.

Before resorting to judicial review, the professional should first exhaust the internal appeal processes provided by the regulatory body, including any professional tribunals or appeal committees designated for such disputes. Only if these channels fail to resolve the issue fairly should judicial review be considered as a possible next step.

3. Illegality as a Ground for Judicial Review

When challenging the legality of a decision or action taken by a public body, the claimant must demonstrate that the authority has not adhered to legal requirements governing its decision-making process.

Illegality, as a ground for judicial review, can manifest in various ways, each relating to the misuse or misunderstanding of the legal framework by the decision-maker.

The following aspects outline how illegality can be identified:

(a) **Error of Law:** The decision-maker has misinterpreted or applied the law incorrectly in reaching their decision.

(b) **Error of Fact:** A decision is based on a factual error, where the incorrect fact was a material (significant) one that influenced the outcome.

(c) **Ultra Vires Actions (Beyond Powers):** The public body has acted beyond the powers granted to it by law or has used its powers for an unauthorised purpose.

(d) **Irrelevant Considerations:** The decision-maker has allowed factors that should not have been considered to influence the decision or has failed to consider relevant factors.

(e) **Fettering Discretion:** The public body has unlawfully restricted its own discretion through a policy or rule, not allowing for exceptions or individual judgement in cases where it should.

(f) **Unlawful Delegation:** The decision-making authority has unlawfully delegated its powers to another body or individual when it was required to exercise them personally.

(g) **Failure to Fulfil a Duty:** The public body has neglected to perform a legal duty or obligation inherent to its function.

For a judicial review claim to be viable, it is essential for the claimant to clearly articulate which aspect of illegality is at issue and provide evidence to substantiate the claim of illegal action or decision-making.

3.1 Ultra Vires Actions

When a public authority operates beyond the scope of the authority conferred upon them by a statute, this is referred to as acting ultra vires or 'beyond their powers'.

The determination of whether a specific action is within the permitted boundaries is a matter of interpreting the statute that bestows the relevant powers.

Consider a scenario where a local education authority is empowered by statute to subsidise student transportation for educational purposes. If the authority extends these subsidies to cover leisure travel for students, such an action would likely be deemed ultra vires. The statute's provisions were intended solely for educational transport, not for broader travel purposes.

As such, by offering subsidies for non-educational travel, the authority would be acting beyond its legally granted powers, rendering its actions illegal.

3.2 Misinterpretation of Legal Principles

Public authorities are often vested with powers to make decisions according to statutes which might contain clauses seemingly protecting these decisions from legal challenges—for example, stating that "decisions made under this act are final and not subject to judicial review."

These provisions, known as ouster clauses, are designed to exclude the courts' supervisory role and can lead to conflicts with the principle of the rule of law, which suggests that legal accountability should not be circumvented.

The judiciary has historically interpreted such clauses with considerable scrutiny, asserting that clauses cannot shield decisions that are fundamentally flawed or made without legal basis. In essence, the courts maintain their authority to review decisions to ensure they are legally valid. If a decision is found to be based on an erroneous understanding of the law, then it is not protected by the ouster clause and may be subject to judicial review.

This preserves the judiciary's role in upholding the rule of law by ensuring that public authorities exercise their powers within the bounds of legality.

3.3 Compliance with Legal Duties

Statutory duties imposed on public authorities stipulate that certain considerations must be factored into their decision-making processes. Notably, the Public Sector Equality Duty compels public entities to consider the impact of their decisions on equality.

(a) **Public Sector Equality Duty.** This duty mandates public authorities to consciously contemplate the need to:

• Eradicate discrimination against those with protected characteristics;

- Promote equal opportunities and nurture harmonious relations among individuals with and without protected characteristics;

- Mitigate or eliminate disadvantages experienced by those with protected characteristics.

Protected characteristics encompass aspects such as age, disability, gender reassignment, pregnancy and maternity, race, religion or belief, sex, and sexual orientation. "Due regard" implies that these considerations must be integrated into the decision-making process, although it does not prescribe a specific outcome.

A local education authority implemented a new policy to amalgamate several schools, which would lead to the discontinuation of a language immersion program for ethnic minority students. The authority did not adequately consider the program's role in supporting the cultural and educational needs of the minority community.

A judicial review found that the authority had not fulfilled its duty to consider the potential negative impact on the educational attainment of the minority students, thus breaching the Public Sector Equality Duty.

3.4 Unauthorised Power Delegation

Legislative provisions often allocate specific responsibilities to designated authorities or officials, which cannot be further delegated unless explicitly permitted by the originating statute. This ensures that the exercise of power remains accountable and traceable to a lawful source.

For instance, an authority empowered by statute may not pass on its decision-making rights to another entity or individual without the statute's direct endorsement. This principle upholds the integrity of the power's original delegation.

A Ministry, endowed with statutory authority to sanction educational grants, outsources its grant allocation process to a private company. This company, in turn, delegates the final grant decision-making to a panel of external consultants.

Such an act would constitute unlawful delegation since the statutory power was explicitly vested in the Ministry and not intended for further distribution to external parties.

3.5 Relevant Considerations

A public body is obliged to make decisions based on factors that are pertinent to the legislation under which they operate. Decisions should be guided solely by considerations that the law recognises as significant to the matter at hand.

Consider a scenario where a government agency is em-powered to allocate funds for urban development projects. If the agency bases its funding decisions on the potential pop-ularity of the project amongst voters, rather than its impact on urban improvement, it has taken into account an irrelevant consideration.

The agency's remit is to assess projects based on their con-tribution to urban development, not their electoral appeal.

4. The Notion of Procedural Impropriety in Judicial Review

Procedural impropriety in judicial review relates to the manner in which a decision has been made. This ground for review is based on the premise that a public authority must adhere to both the procedural rules set out in legislation and the common law when making decisions.

Instances of procedural impropriety can occur when:

(a) **Statutory procedural requirements are not met;**

(b) **Common law principles of natural justice, such as the right to a fair hearing, are violated; or**

(c) **There is evidence of bias or a lack of impartiality in the decision-making process.**

The following discussion elaborates on these aspects of procedural impropriety.

4.1 Mandatory vs. Directory Procedural Requirements

Procedural requirements in legislation are categorised as either mandatory or directory. A mandatory requirement is one that a public authority must strictly adhere to, and failure to do so typically invalidates the decision made.

Conversely, non-compliance with a directory requirement does not automatically invalidate a decision, although it may still affect the legality of the decision depending on the context and potential impact on those involved.

If a government department neglects to consult with a statutory advisory body as mandated by law before implementing a new environmental regulation, such oversight could be grounds for the regulation's invalidity due to non-observance of a mandatory procedural requirement.

4.2 Common Law Procedural Requirements

Beyond statutory requirements, public authorities must also comply with procedural standards developed under common law, including the principles of natural justice which encompass the following:

(a) **Right to Be Heard.** The principle of the right to be heard demands that individuals or parties affected by a decision have the opportunity to present their case.

The scope of this right varies, but it generally includes the chance to be informed of the case against oneself and the opportunity to offer a counter-argument, especially in situations where rights or interests are at risk of being adversely affected.

(b) **Rule Against Bias.** Common law insists that decision-makers must be free from bias, which can manifest in several forms:

- **Actual Bias:** Direct evidence of bias influencing a decision, which is typically hard to prove.

- **Automatic Disqualification Rule:** A decision-maker is automatically disqualified from making a decision if they have a financial or other substantial interest in the outcome.

- **Apparent Bias:** The perception of bias based on circumstances that might lead a reasonable observer to question the impartiality of the decision-maker.

For instance, a planning officer deciding on a property development application might be perceived as biassed if they own property nearby, potentially benefiting from the development's impact on property values.

(c) **Duty to Consult.** Under common law, there isn't a blanket obligation for public bodies to engage in consultation processes; however, specific circumstances can trigger the duty to consult. This duty is typically not a default requirement because of the potential to hinder the efficiency of governmental decision-making processes.

Nevertheless, situations where this duty may be invoked include:

- **Instances** where legislation expressly mandates consultation before taking certain actions or making decisions;

- **Scenarios** where a public authority has pledged to undertake consultation, creating an expectation that they will seek input before proceeding;

- **Cases** where a history of consultation exists, establishing a consistent practice that stakeholders anticipate will continue; and

- **Unusual cases** where the lack of consultation would result in notably unfair outcomes, compelling the public authority to consult in the interest of equity and justice.

For instance, if a local council has routinely consulted with neighbourhood associations before initiating zoning changes, it would be expected to continue this practice for new zoning proposals to avoid claims of unfairness.

(d) Duty to Give Reasons. Under common law, public authorities are not universally obliged to explain their decisions. This principle avoids administrative processes becoming overly cumbersome. Nevertheless, there are certain instances when providing an explanation is deemed necessary for the sake of fairness:

- In matters of significant consequence, such as those affecting individual freedoms, it is only fair for the affected parties to understand the rationale behind the decisions that impact them.

- If a decision deviates markedly from what would normally be anticipated, fairness dictates that an explanation is provided to allow those affected to determine if there has been a mistake or oversight that warrants legal challenge.

If an employee in a public sector role is abruptly dismissed after a long tenure and awarded a seemingly inadequate severance package, there is a common law expectation for the reasoning behind both the dismissal and the amount of compensation to be articulated.

This is to ensure that the decision is transparent and the employee has the opportunity to contest it if there appears to be an error or misjudgment.

5. The Concept of Legitimate Expectations in Public Administration

A legitimate expectation in legal terms is created when a public body's actions or assurances lead individuals or groups to anticipate that it will act in a certain way. There are two primary ways through which a legitimate expectation can be established:

(a)   Through a clear promise or **declaration by the public authority**.

(b)   Through a **consistent pattern of past behaviour** that sets a precedent.

When such an expectation is established, the courts may compel the public authority to honour that expectation, unless to do so would be unlawful or override a stronger public interest.

This expectation could relate to a procedural right, such as the right to be consulted, or it could pertain to a specific substantive benefit or policy made known to the public.

A university publicly announces a scholarship program for students from low-income backgrounds, outlining specific eligibility criteria on its website. Based on this information, a student, Alex, who meets all the published criteria, applies for the scholarship and plans her finances around the expectation of receiving this support. However, when the scholarships are awarded, the university denies Alex's application based on additional criteria that were never made public.

Alex has a legitimate expectation that the university will assess her application based on the criteria that were publicly announced. By introducing new, undisclosed criteria, the university has breached this expectation. If Alex were to challenge the university's decision, a court might require the university to reassess her application based solely on the original, published criteria, unless the university can demonstrate a lawful reason or an overriding public interest for the change in policy that was not previously disclosed.

5.1 Precedence as a Basis for Legitimate Expectation

The historical actions of a public body can also create a legitimate expectation.

For the past decade, a local education authority had a practice of offering grants to all students achieving a set grade threshold in their A-Level examinations to support their university education. Based on this, students like Sophia worked diligently to meet the threshold, expecting to receive the grant.

However, the authority abruptly discontinued the grant program without prior notification. This sudden change, without any consultation or transitional arrangements, could be seen as a violation of the legitimate expectation of the students who had relied on the established practice of the authority.

5.2 Substantive Versus Procedural Legitimate Expectations

Occasionally, a legitimate expectation extends beyond procedural aspects, becoming substantial when a public authority's promise holds significant weight and is directed at a limited group of individuals.

In a small rural community, the local council had offered a grant scheme to support the restoration of historic buildings, promising specific funding amounts to applicants like Mr. Thompson, who owned a Grade II listed cottage. Relying on this pledge, Mr. Thompson began extensive restoration works. Later, the council attempted to withdraw the funding due to budget cuts.

However, the courts may hold the council to its original commitment, given the substantial investment Mr. Thompson made based on the council's promise, which was directed at a distinct and small group of property owners. The financial implications for the council would likely be secondary to the importance of maintaining the trust and reliance placed on its explicit assurances.

6. The Thresholds of Unreasonableness and Irrationality in Decision-Making

When a decision by a public authority is so devoid of any plausible justification that it borders on the absurd or defies logic, it may be deemed irrational or unreasonable.

This concept encapsulates decisions that no sensible authority, upon proper consideration, could ever endorse. The threshold for establishing irrationality is notably high, as the judiciary generally shows deference to the judgement of administrative authorities.

Consider a scenario where a local housing authority denies a renovation grant to Mr. Johnson, an eligible applicant, solely because he supports a different football team than the members of the grant approval committee.

Such a decision could be challenged on the grounds of irrationality, as the preference for a football team bears no logical relation to the criteria for grant eligibility and flies in the face of common sense.

6.1 Proportionality in Human Rights and European Union Law

In circumstances where decisions impinge upon rights safeguarded by the Human Rights Act 1998 or formerly by EU law, the stringent threshold of unreasonableness is supplanted by the 'proportionality' test. This test is also pertinent for rights acknowledged under common law, independent of the Human Rights Act.

The proportionality test entails a meticulous scrutiny comprising three steps:

(a) **Legitimate Aim:** The decision must pursue a goal of sufficient importance to warrant the encroachment of a fundamental right.

(b) **Rational Connection:** The measures employed must be logically connected to the objective sought by the legislation or policy.

(c) **Least Restrictive Means:** The limitation of the right should be no more intrusive than what is necessary to achieve the legislative goal.

7. Judicial Remedies

Upon establishing the grounds for a judicial review, the court has several remedies at its disposal to rectify the situation.

These legal correctives include:

(a) **Quashing Order:** This nullifies the impugned decision, essentially erasing it from the record as though it never existed, compelling the public body to reassess the matter.

(b) **Mandatory Order:** This compels the public body to execute a particular act it is obliged to perform under the law.

(c) **Prohibiting Order (Prohibition):** This prevents a public body from acting or continuing an action that exceeds its lawful jurisdiction.

(d) **Injunction:** Similar to its function in private law, an injunction can either restrain a public body from a particular action or mandate that it follows certain directives outlined by the court.

(e) **Declaration:** This is a statement from the court affirming the legality or illegality of an action or decision, clarifying the legal position without necessarily ordering any party to act.

While quashing, mandatory, and prohibiting orders are exclusive to the judicial review process, injunctions and declarations share the same characteristics and functions as in private law contexts.

7.1 Combining Remedies for Comprehensive Justice

The court has the discretion to issue combined remedies in a judicial review to ensure comprehensive redress. A typical example might see the original decision annulled with a quashing order, while a mandatory order may compel the public authority to reassess the matter in adherence to legal standards. This could result in a different outcome or potentially lead to the same decision if the authority's reconsideration is free from the initial legal flaw.

Let's consider Michaela, whose permit to operate a burger stand in the local marketplace was rescinded by the municipal council. The decision was made by Trevor, a competing vendor who also sells burgers and who claimed Michaela's stand caused excessive littering. Michaela challenges the decision on the grounds of Trevor's bias.

The court, finding the bias claim valid, issues a quashing order, invalidating the original decision. The council is then mandated to revisit the decision lawfully. If upon review — this time conducted without bias — the council reaches the same decision based on the littering issue, the new decision stands legally.

7.2 The Discretionary Nature of Remedies

Remedies in judicial review are not guaranteed outcomes but are at the discretion of the courts. A successful claim does not automatically result in a remedy being granted.

The court may choose not to issue a remedy if it believes that doing so would not alter the situation in a meaningful way, or if third parties have acted in reliance on the decision in question.

Consider the scenario where the head of the Monopolies and Mergers Commission unilaterally decides not to pursue an inquiry into a merger, a move that is procedurally incorrect as the decision should have been collective.

Despite the procedural error, the court opts not to issue a remedy because it is anticipated that the full commission would arrive at the same decision if the process were repeated, and because relevant third parties had already commenced actions based on the initial decision.

CHAPTER 9. THE HUMAN RIGHTS ACT OF 1998

1. The Dynamic Relationship between the European Convention on Human Rights and the Human Rights Act 1998

The European Convention on Human Rights, ratified by the United Kingdom in the mid-20th century, is an international treaty designed to safeguard fundamental rights and freedoms. Under its terms, individuals can ultimately appeal to the European Court of Human Rights if they believe their rights under the Convention have been violated, once all domestic legal avenues have been exhausted. The Court's judgments are legally binding on the country concerned.

To facilitate the domestic enforcement of these rights, the UK passed the Human Rights Act in 1998, which effectively weaved the Convention rights into the fabric of British law. This act empowers UK courts to hear cases and provide remedies related to human rights issues as defined by the ECHR, without the immediate need for individuals to seek recourse from the Strasbourg court.

This section will explore the ECHR's key tenets and the application of the HRA within the context of the UK's legal framework.

2. Dissecting HRA Section 1— the Incorporation of the Convention's Rights into Domestic Law

Section 1 of the Human Rights Act (HRA) 1998 enshrines a set of rights and freedoms from the European Convention on Human Rights (ECHR) into UK law. These rights are divided into various categories based on the extent to which they may be subject to restrictions by the state.

2.1 Absolute Rights

Absolute rights are those that the state cannot infringe upon or restrict, regardless of the circumstances. These rights are unequivocal, and no exceptions or conditions can justify their breach.

Examples of absolute rights include the prohibition of torture and inhuman or degrading treatment or punishment. These rights must be upheld at all times, reflecting their foundational significance in a democratic society.

2.2 Exploring Limited Rights

Certain rights recognised by the HRA are not absolute but can be limited or restricted under specific circumstances which are clearly defined within the ECHR itself.

These rights, known as 'limited rights', are circumscribed to particular instances and procedural requirements set out in the relevant articles. An example of a limited right is the right to liberty and security, as detailed in Article 5 of the ECHR.

It permits the deprivation of liberty under distinct conditions, such as:

(a) The **lawful detention** of a person after conviction by a competent court.

(b) **Lawful arrest** or detention of individuals who have not complied with a court order or to ensure the fulfilment of an obligation prescribed by law.

(c) **Lawful arrest or detention** of individuals reasonably suspected of wrongdoing or to prevent them from committing an offence.

(d) **Detention** under the law for the spread prevention of infectious diseases, the detention of those who are mentally ill, and others specified under Article 5.

These restrictions highlight that while the right to liberty and security is a fundamental human right, it can be lawfully curtailed under specific, controlled circumstances, ensuring a balance between individual freedoms and public or social interests.

2.3 The Scope of Qualified Rights

Qualified rights under the Human Rights Act 1998 are those rights which can be subject to certain restrictions by the state. These limitations are permissible provided they are in accordance with the law, pursue a legitimate aim as outlined within the specific article of the European Convention on Human Rights (ECHR), and are necessary in a democratic society.

(a) **Article 10—Freedom of Expression.** Article 10 of the European Convention on Human Rights enshrines the right to freedom of expression, encompassing the liberty to hold views and to disseminate and receive information and ideas without unwarranted interference by public authorities.

Nonetheless, this provision also acknowledges that such freedom may be subject to constraints as dictated by law and as necessary within the confines of a democratic society, for objectives such as safeguarding national security, maintaining territorial integrity, ensuring public safety, preventing disorder or crime, and protecting health or morals.

Consider the scenario where an individual openly endorses a recognised terrorist group and disseminates online content encouraging others to engage in acts of terrorism to promote the group's objectives.

If law enforcement apprehends and prosecutes this individual for inciting terrorism, the limitation imposed on their freedom of expression is legally justified and crucial for the protection of national security.

Consequently, this limitation would be in alignment with the stipulations of Article 10.

(b) **Article 11—Freedom of Assembly and Association.** Article 11 of the European Convention on Human Rights guarantees the right to peaceful assembly and to freedom of association with others, including the right to form and to join trade unions for the protection of one's interests. Nevertheless, it acknowledges the possibility of legal restrictions on these freedoms, provided such restrictions are deemed necessary in a democratic society for objectives such as safeguarding national security, preventing disorder or crime, protecting health or morals, or securing the rights and freedoms of others.

Consider a scenario where a group plans a demonstration that is expected to incite violence or disrupt public order. The authorities might impose certain conditions on the demonstration or, in extreme cases, prohibit it entirely.

Such restrictions, while a limitation on the right to freedom of assembly, would be legally valid if they are proportionate, prescribed by law, and necessary to meet one of the legitimate aims set out in Article 11, such as preventing disorder or protecting the rights and freedoms of others.

(c) **Other Qualified Rights.** Other qualified rights, similar to Articles 10 and 11 concerning freedom of expression and assembly, are contingent on certain conditions and may be subject to lawful restrictions. These rights are not absolute and can be limited by the state to protect various public interests and the rights of others.

- Article 8 guarantees the right to respect for private and family life, one's home, and correspondence. However, public authorities can interfere with this right if it is in accordance with the law and necessary for objectives such as national security, public safety, economic well-being, prevention of disorder or crime, protection of health or morals, or protection of the rights and freedoms of others.

-

- Article 9 provides the right to freedom of thought, conscience, and religion, which includes the freedom to change one's religion or belief and to manifest one's religion or belief. Restrictions may be applied for the protection of public order, health, or morals, or the protection of the rights and freedoms of others.

These restrictions must be lawful, pursue a legitimate aim, and be necessary in a democratic society, meaning they must be proportionate and relevant to the aims they seek to achieve.

The European Court of Human Rights has developed a substantial body of case law interpreting these rights and the conditions under which they can be restricted, emphasising the importance of balancing individual rights with the interests of the community.

2.4 The Principle of Proportionality

When it comes to curtailing a qualified right, the state's intervention must be necessary and proportionate to the sought-after legitimate aim. This assessment is conducted through a tripartite proportionality test employed by the courts, which scrutinises whether the policy's objective justifies the infringement of a fundamental right, if the measure in question is suitably designed to achieve its goal, and whether the limitation imposed is the least intrusive means necessary to realise the stated objective.

Consider a situation where a city imposes a curfew during a period of unrest to maintain public order. If challenged, a court would assess the proportionality of the curfew by considering whether maintaining public order (the legitimate aim) justifies the restriction of the right to freedom of movement.

The court would evaluate if the curfew directly contributes to the maintenance of order and if the restriction is the least intrusive means available. If it turns out that the curfew is too broad in scope or duration, making it more restrictive than necessary, it may be deemed disproportionate and thus unlawful.

2.5 Judicial Deference

Judicial deference refers to the discretion that courts often exercise to respect the expertise and judgement of the legislative or executive branches on matters where those branches are considered to have greater expertise, especially in politically sensitive areas.

If a government enacts legislation restricting certain forms of protest in the interest of national security, courts may show deference to the government's assessment of what is required for national security, acknowledging that the executive has access to security intelligence and expertise that the courts do not.

In such cases, provided that the government can reasonably justify the restriction as necessary for the protection of national security, courts are likely to uphold the measure, even if it would, under less sensitive circumstances, demand a more stringent examination of its proportionality and necessity.

2.6 The Margin of Appreciation Doctrine

When facing challenges before the ECtHR, the UK government may invoke a 'margin of appreciation,' essentially a leeway given to national authorities in determining the extent of restriction necessary on a qualified right, in light of the cultural, historical, and societal context of the state.

The margin of appreciation doctrine acknowledges that national authorities, by virtue of their direct contact and familiarisation with the society, are in a better position to make such decisions, as opposed to an international tribunal.

The interplay between the European Convention on Human Rights and the Human Rights Act of 1998 showcases the UK's commitment to safeguarding human rights. The Act's structure emphasises a nuanced balance between protection of individual rights and the acknowledgement of national interests, maintaining a dynamic relationship with the ECHR that is both respectful of sovereignty and compliant with international human rights standards.

For law students and practitioners, this chapter underscores the importance of a comprehensive understanding of how these rights are implemented and adjudicated, both at the domestic level and within the European human rights framework.

2.7 The Living Instrument Principle and Its Implications

The "living instrument" doctrine adopted by the European Court of Human Rights (ECtHR) refers to the notion that the European Convention on Human Rights (ECHR) should be interpreted in light of present-day conditions and norms, rather than being restricted to the intentions of its drafters at the time of its creation.

This dynamic approach allows the Convention to remain relevant and responsive to the evolution of society, ensuring that its protections are effective and meaningful in the contemporary context.

This principle is supported by a few key sub-principles:

(a) Flexibility in Precedent Adherence

The European Court of Human Rights (ECtHR) operates with a certain degree of judicial flexibility, as it is not strictly bound by its previous decisions.

This flexibility is important because it allows the Court to reassess its jurisprudence in light of new circumstances or emerging human rights norms. While the principle of legal certainty and consistency means that past decisions are given considerable weight, the ECtHR retains the ability to adapt and evolve its interpretations of the European Convention on Human Rights (ECHR).

This can occur when novel issues emerge that were not contemplated in earlier rulings or when there is a significant shift in societal values or international legal standards that warrants a different approach.

Such a dynamic interpretive method ensures that the protection of human rights under the ECHR continues to be effective and relevant in an ever-changing world.

(b) Consistency with Contracting States' Approaches

The European Court of Human Rights (ECtHR) may observe and incorporate the practices and legal standards common among the contracting states when interpreting the provisions of the European Convention on Human Rights (ECHR). If there is a consistent approach or consensus on a particular issue among member states, the Court may be inclined to align its judgments with this common understanding.

This collective approach can influence the Court to deviate from its earlier decisions, especially when these common practices reflect a contemporary and harmonised perspective on human rights matters. By doing so, the ECtHR ensures that its jurisprudence is in step with the prevailing legal and societal norms across Europe, which reinforces the relevance and applicability of the ECHR in diverse legal systems.

(c) Accessibility and Relevance of the ECtHR

The European Court of Human Rights (ECtHR) approaches the interpretation of the European Convention on Human Rights (ECHR) with the principle that its protections must be realistically available to all individuals. This notion of accessibility ensures that the rights enshrined in the Convention are not theoretical or illusory but are genuine and effective.

For instance, in a landmark case, the ECtHR held that prisoners retain certain fundamental rights despite their incarceration. The Court found that prohibiting prisoners from consulting with legal representatives infringed upon their right to a fair trial as guaranteed under Article 6 of the Convention. This decision underscored the Court's commitment to ensuring that individuals can practically exercise their Convention rights, even in the context of imprisonment, where certain liberties are necessarily curtailed.

2.8 The Concept of Derogation Under the ECHR

In exceptional cases, specifically when a nation faces dire threats such as warfare or a national crisis jeopardising its stability, a government is permitted to temporarily suspend certain obligations under the European Convention on Human Rights (ECHR).

This is known as a derogation. However, there are strict limitations on this prerogative:

(a) **Derogation Limitations.** Certain fundamental rights are insulated from derogation. These include the prohibition of torture and inhumane treatment (Article 3), the ban on slavery and forced labor (Article 4(1)), and the protection against retroactive criminal laws (Article 7).

(b) **Circumstances Permitting Derogation.** Derogation is permissible only in extreme scenarios such as war or a public emergency that imperils the nation's survival.

(c) **Scope of Derogation.** Any deviation from the conventional rights must be narrowly tailored to the demands of the situation, without exceeding what is strictly necessary to address the emergency.

3. The Role of Section 2 of the HRA in Interpreting Convention Rights

Section 2 of the Human Rights Act 1998 mandates that UK courts, when deliberating on matters concerning rights enshrined in the Convention, must give due consideration to the relevant jurisprudence of the European Court of Human Rights (ECtHR). This does not bind UK courts to follow the ECtHR decisions rigidly, but they are expected to regard the ECtHR's interpretations as highly persuasive, particularly when a consistent line of decisions exists.

This principle is encapsulated in the concept often referred to as the 'mirror principle', which advocates for a harmonious reflection of ECtHR jurisprudence in UK court rulings. The rationale is to ensure that the protection of human rights under the Convention is applied uniformly, providing neither less nor more protection than what the ECtHR has established. This creates a synergy between the national courts' interpretation of Convention rights and the ECtHR's jurisprudence, upholding the intention behind the incorporation of the ECHR into UK law via the Human Rights Act.

4. The HRA's Section 3 and Its Impact on Legislation Interpretation

Section 3 of the Human Rights Act 1998 places a duty on UK courts to interpret domestic legislation in a manner that is consistent with the rights stipulated in the European Convention on Human Rights, to the extent that such an interpretation is feasible.

This powerful interpretative obligation often requires courts to read and give effect to the statutes in a way that aligns with the principles enshrined in the Convention, sometimes even if this means stretching the conventional meanings of words and phrases within the legislation.

Take, for example, a scenario where a law protects the dwelling rights of tenants who are bereaved of their partners, specifically defining a partner as a 'husband or wife.'

This definition, on the face of it, does not extend to unmarried cohabiting couples. If a woman named Jane, who has been living with her partner in a long-term, stable relationship, faces eviction following her partner's death, she could argue that the narrow statutory definition fails to protect her right to respect for her home and family life under Article 8 and her right to non-discrimination under Article 14 of the ECHR.

Using the interpretative powers granted by Section 3, a court could read the statute to include long-term cohabiting partners within its ambit, ensuring the domestic law aligns with Convention rights.

5. Section 4 and Declarations of Incompatibility

Section 4 of the Human Rights Act 1998 empowers UK courts to issue a declaration of incompatibility when it is unfeasible to interpret a statute or subordinate legislation in a manner that is consistent with the rights enshrined in the European Convention on Human Rights.

Such a declaration, however, does not nullify the legislation in question due to the doctrine of parliamentary sovereignty.

Therefore, the legislation remains enforceable, but the declaration signals to the government and Parliament the potential need for legislative amendment.

Consider the case where the current legal provisions unequivocally restrict a certain group of individuals, such as those with a specific disability, from obtaining a driver's licence, without considering individual circumstances.

This could potentially conflict with Article 14 (Prohibition of Discrimination) in conjunction with Article 8 (Right to Respect for Private and Family Life). If a court finds it impossible to interpret these provisions in a way that respects these Convention rights, it may issue a declaration of incompatibility, recommending that Parliament revisit and potentially revise the legislation.

However, until such legislative changes are made, the original statutory prohibition remains in effect.

5.1 Addressing Incompatibilities

Legislation deemed incompatible with Convention rights can be amended or repealed through standard legislative procedures. However, to expedite minor adjustments that might otherwise be bogged down in the legislative process, Section 10 of the HRA provides expedited mechanisms for rectifying such incompatibilities, with specific provisions for both non-urgent and urgent situations.

(a) **The Remedial Order Process for Non-Urgent Corrections.** For non-urgent amendments, Section 10 allows for a "remedial order," a form of secondary legislation that can modify primary legislation or other secondary legislation. Such an order becomes law after 60 days of draft publication, pending approval by both the House of Commons and the House of Lords.

(b) The Expedited Process for Urgent Corrections. In urgent cases, a remedial order can be enacted immediately by a government minister and take immediate effect. The order must subsequently be presented to Parliament and will lapse if not approved within 120 days.

6. Section 6 and Its Enforcement Against Public Authorities

Section 6 of the HRA makes it unlawful for public authorities to act in ways that contravene Convention rights, effectively establishing a new statutory basis for judicial review centred on human rights.

This section encompasses a broad range of entities performing public functions, with certain exclusions specified within the Act itself.

6.1 Clarifying the Definition of a Public Authority

A public authority, as defined by the HRA, includes any entity performing functions of a public nature, such as government departments and local authorities.

However, the legislation explicitly excludes the legislative bodies of the House of Commons and the House of Lords from this definition.

6.2 Further Exclusions and Conditions

Actions by public authorities are not deemed unlawful under Section 6 if the authority could not have acted differently without violating the letter of an Act of Parliament.

If the authority's actions were in direct compliance with primary legislation that cannot be interpreted compatible with Convention rights, the authority's conduct is not unlawful, and a declaration of incompatibility may instead be issued under Section 4.

7. Section 7 and Legal Proceedings Against Public Authorities

Section 7 of the Human Rights Act 1998 (HRA) delineates the legal framework for initiating legal proceedings against public authorities accused of breaching the rights set forth in the European Convention on Human Rights (ECHR). Central to this process is the requirement that the individual bringing forth the claim must be a 'victim' of the purported unlawful act by the public authority.

The term 'victim' is construed narrowly under the HRA, as opposed to the broader standing typically required for judicial review. This means that the individual must have been directly affected by the action in question. Thus, cases cannot be brought by third-party organisations on behalf of others, unless they too have been directly impacted.

Moreover, the HRA stipulates a strict time frame for these legal actions. Claims must be initiated within one year from the date of the event that is alleged to have violated the claimant's human rights. This period can only be extended if the court finds it equitable to do so, based on the specific circumstances of the case.

Jamie, an amateur photographer, is stopped by the police while taking pictures in a public space. The officers confiscate his camera, claiming it's for security reasons, without providing any legal basis for their actions. This leaves Jamie unable to continue his photography and feeling that his rights under Article 10 of the ECHR (freedom of expression) have been violated.

In this situation, Jamie would have the right to bring a case under Section 7 of the HRA as he is the 'victim' of the action – his personal rights have been directly infringed by the public authority's actions. Jamie must file his claim within one year of the confiscation of his camera.

On the other hand, if a civil liberties organisation that advocates for the rights of photographers wants to challenge the police's actions on Jamie's behalf, they wouldn't be considered a 'victim' under the HRA because they were not directly affected by the police's conduct. They could potentially provide support or advice to Jamie, but they could not be the primary claimants in an action under Section 7. Only Jamie, whose rights were directly impinged upon, could take this step, providing he does so within the one-year time frame.

8. Section 8 and Available Remedies

Under Section 8 of the Human Rights Act 1998, should a claim against a public authority, as outlined in Section 6, prove successful, UK courts hold discretionary powers to determine suitable remedies.

These remedies are designed to be just and fitting to the case at hand. In essence, the court has the autonomy to decide whether to grant a remedy and which of the available judicial review remedies to apply.

In instances where the court possesses the authority to award damages, such authority extends to claims brought under Section 6.

However, the court must judiciously consider the availability of alternative remedies and adhere to the guiding principles established by the European Court of Human Rights' case law when deciding on the awarding of damages.

9. Combating Discrimination Through the ECHR and the Equality Act 2010

9.1 Article 14 of the ECHR and the Prohibition of Discrimination

Article 14 enshrines the principle that the rights and freedoms set forth in the Convention must be secured without discrimination on any ground, including sex, race, colour, language, political or other opinions, national or social origin, association with a national minority, property, birth, or other status. Both direct and indirect forms of discrimination fall under this prohibition.

(a) **The Restricted Scope of Article 14.** Claims of discrimination under the HRA must be tethered to the infringement of another Convention right. Standalone discrimination claims are not permissible under the HRA, highlighting the integrative nature of Article 14's protections.

Consider an individual with a physical disability who is denied access to a public building due to a lack of suitable facilities, which are available for able-bodied individuals. If this individual is contesting the right to access public services—a right related to the broader scope of the ECHR rights—they might also raise a claim of discrimination under Article 14, arguing that their right to, say, freedom of assembly (Article 11) is being infringed upon in a discriminatory manner due to their disability.

(b) **The 'Living Instrument' Approach.** In line with the 'living instrument' principle, the ECtHR has interpreted the ECHR's provisions, including Article 14, in a manner that reflects evolving societal values and norms. The term 'other status' has been expansively construed to encompass categories such as sexual orientation, marital status, and asylum seeker status, thereby broadening the ambit of Article 14's anti-discrimination mandate.

(c) **The Narrow Margin of Appreciation in Discrimination Matters.** In matters relating to Article 14, the ECtHR affords states only a limited margin of appreciation. This constricted latitude underscores the rigorous scrutiny applied to discriminatory practices, underscoring the ECtHR's commitment to upholding equality and preventing discrimination.

9.2 The Equality Act 2010 and Its Additional Safeguards

The Equality Act 2010 supplements the anti-discrimination protections of Article 14, prohibiting discrimination on the grounds of protected characteristics, such as age, disability, gender reassignment, race, religion or belief, sex, sexual orientation, marriage and civil partnership, and pregnancy and maternity.

(a) **Distinctive Features of the Equality Act 2010.** In contrast to Article 14, the Equality Act permits standalone discrimination claims, independent of other rights, providing a direct avenue for redress in cases of discriminatory conduct.

(b) **b. Eligibility to Pursue Claims Under the Equality Act 2010.** Within the employment sector, individuals categorised as 'workers' can initiate claims against employers or organisations under the Act. Significantly, the Act's provisions are not confined to public bodies, extending protections to private sector employment as well.

(c) **Varied Forms of Discrimination Addressed by the Act.** The Act explicitly outlaws direct discrimination, indirect discrimination, harassment, and victimisation, defining each form of discrimina-

tion and setting the parameters for lawful and unlawful conduct.

- **Direct Discrimination:** Occurs when an individual is subjected to less favourable treatment
  because of a protected characteristic.

A gentleman is denied membership to a local book club after
revealing his sexual orientation. If the club's policy is to exclude individuals based on their sexual orientation, this would
represent a clear case of direct discrimination.

- **Indirect discrimination:** Indirect discrimination takes place when a universal policy, practice,
  or rule is implemented across the board but disproportionately disadvantages a specific protected
  group. However, not all such instances are
  deemed indirect discrimination. If the policy in
  question is justified as being necessary and proportionate to achieve a legitimate and rational
  aim, this is referred to as 'objective justification,'
  and the policy may be exempt from being classified as discriminatory.

A corporate firm enforces a policy requiring all employees to work on Saturdays. This policy disproportionately affects Jewish employees who observe the Sabbath. Should the firm demonstrate that the Saturday work policy is crucial for its operations and no reasonable alternative is available, it could potentially defend the policy as objectively justifiable.

- **Harassment:** Harassment is identified when an individual experiences behaviour that is not welcomed, and this behaviour is intended or has the effect of creating an environment that is intimidating, hostile, degrading, humiliating, or offensive for the individual. Such conduct is inherently unjustifiable and is considered unlawful as it violates the individual's dignity and creates an adverse environment for them.

An employee with a physical disability is subject to continuous jokes about their condition from colleagues, leading to a distressing work environment. Both the employer and the individuals engaging in this conduct would be held accountable for harassment.

- **Victimisation:** Victimisation is characterised by adverse treatment directed at an individual who has lodged a complaint about discrimination or has assisted someone else in making such a complaint. This treatment could be in the form of penalisation, retaliation, or other negative consequences as a result of their actions in standing against discrimination. This is unlawful as it punishes individuals for asserting their rights under discrimination laws.

A woman supports her colleague's sexual harassment claim against their manager by providing a statement. Following her involvement, she experiences a sudden demotion. Should it be evident that her demotion was a repercussion of her supportive action, she could have grounds for a victimisation claim.

CHAPTER 10. LAW ON PUBLIC ORDER

1. The Interplay between ECHR and HRA

The ECHR and HRA acknowledge specific rights—referred to as qualified rights—that can be subject to certain restrictions or penalties prescribed by law that are deemed necessary in a democratic society, especially for the protection of national security, public safety, or to prevent disorder or crime.

These rights include the freedom of expression under Article 10 and the freedom of assembly and association under Article 11.

In relation, the Public Order Act 1986 empowers public authorities, especially police, with the authority to limit protest rights and to detain individuals who disrupt public order. Thus, this act and any related legislation that regulate protests must be interpreted in line with the ECHR and HRA.

Let's consider a situation where a group of librarians form a union to protest against reduced funding for public libraries. They decide to organise a peaceful sit-in at a major public library.

However, the police, citing potential disruption to public services and safety concerns due to the anticipated large turnout, restricted the protest to a nearby public park and set conditions on the duration of the protest.

Provided that these restrictions are proportionate and in line with the law, they would be consistent with the limitations allowed under the Public Order Act 1986, which must be interpreted in harmony with the ECHR and HRA.

2. Breach of the Peace

2.1 Upholding the 'Queen's Peace'

The concept of the 'Queen's Peace' is a foundational aspect of the common law in the UK, which obligates police officers to preserve public order. This duty compels the police to safeguard individuals' ability to carry out their daily activities without excessive disturbance from others.

This traditional common law power complements the statutory offences delineated in the Public Order Act 1986, allowing for a flexible and responsive approach to maintaining public tranquillity.

If a protest outside a government building becomes disruptive, with protestors obstructing entry and exit points, the police may intervene to prevent a breach of the peace. They can take action to disperse the crowd or make arrests if necessary to restore order, thereby upholding the 'Queen's Peace'.

2.2 Criteria for a Breach of the Peace

A **breach of the peace** occurs when:

(a)　An **individual genuinely fears harm** to themselves or their property because of an assault, affray, riot, or other forms of disturbance.

(b)　**Actual harm** has been done to a person or to their property in their presence.

(c)　There is a **likelihood of harm to a person** or to property in their presence.

Note that mere verbal insults do not constitute a breach of the peace. The words must be accompanied by conduct that leads someone to believe they are at immediate risk of harm.

2.3 Breach of the Peace in Private and Public

Breaches of the peace are not confined to public areas; they may also transpire on private property, encompassing domestic dwellings.

Case where Jamie is observed outside Alex's residence, loudly banging on the door and threatening to vandalise Alex's car parked in the driveway. Although no actual vandalism has taken place, the threat and aggressive behaviour could constitute a breach of the peace, as Alex has a legitimate fear of impending harm to their property.

2.4 Police Response to Breach of the Peace

Police officers are authorised to take appropriate actions to halt an ongoing breach of the peace or to preclude an imminent one. These measures may include apprehending the individual involved or entering private premises by force if necessary.

During an escalating protest where violence has erupted, law enforcement may employ containment strategies, such as establishing a perimeter around the demonstrators to defuse the situation.

This could potentially last several hours. According to the European Court of Human Rights, such tactics are permissible under the right to liberty if they serve to prevent significant injury or property damage and if law enforcement continually assesses the circumstances. By adhering to these parameters, the authorities aim to safeguard the rights to freedom of expression, assembly, and association.

2.5 Imminence of Harm

For a breach of the peace to justify police intervention, the threat must be immediate or "imminent," meaning it is on the verge of transpiring.

Picture a scenario where a convoy of demonstrators is en route to a protest at a nuclear facility. Previous protests of a similar nature have escalated into significant disorder. Midway to their destination, the police halt the convoy and command the demonstrators to return from whence they came, all under close police escort.

This pre-emptive measure was judged to overstep the police's remit in averting a breach of the peace, as the anticipated disruption was not on the brink of occurrence at the point of police intervention.

2.6 Authority to Impose Binding Over Orders

While a breach of the peace itself does not constitute a criminal offence, an individual implicated in such a breach may be subjected to a binding over order. This legal instrument compels the individual concerned to uphold peaceable conduct and exhibit good behaviour over a designated duration.

3. Regulation of Public Processions

Under the provisions of the Public Order Act 1986, public marches are subject to various stipulations, and under specific circumstances, they may be prohibited entirely.

3.1 Notification Requirement for Processions

Typically, a public procession transpires in a public domain, often on public roads. Prior notification to the police is generally required for processions aimed at:

(a) **Demonstrating support** for or opposition to the views or actions of any person or group;

(b) **Promoting a cause** or campaign; or

(c) **Observing or commemorating an event**, except where it is not reasonably feasible to provide such notice.

3.2 Details of Notification

For a public procession, the following notification criteria must be satisfied:

(a)   The advance notice must be submitted **no less than six clear days prior to the planned date of the procession.** 'Clear days' exclude the day of notice submission and the day of the procession itself, effectively necessitating a minimum one-week notice period.

(b)   The notice must be handed **in at a police station** situated within the vicinity where the procession is intended to occur.

(c)   The notice must **detail the procession's date, time, planned route, and the name and address of the organiser** or one of the organisers.

Failure to comply with these notification conditions constitutes an offence, potentially leading to a financial penalty.

3.3 Exemptions from Notification

Certain types of processions are exempt from the notification requirements:

(a) **Processions** that are traditionally or routinely held, like Remembrance Day parades or established annual religious processions in a community.

(b) **Funeral processions** that are organised by funeral directors as part of their professional services.

3.4 Authority to Impose Conditions on Processions

Upon receiving notification of a planned march, the ranking police officer—typically the area's Chief Constable or the highest-ranking officer on-site—has the authority to set specific conditions regarding the march's details if they believe:

(a) **The event may lead to serious disruption,** property damage, or significant disturbance to the community's routine; or

(b) **The march's intent is to coerce others** either to perform an act they are legally entitled to refrain from or to abstain from an act they are legally entitled to undertake;

In such instances, the officer can prescribe any necessary stipulations to avert the anticipated issues. These can dictate the march's trajectory and might include barring the procession from certain public areas.

3.5 Legal Ramifications for Non-compliance

Should the organisers or participants knowingly fail to adhere to imposed conditions, or incite others to violate these conditions during the procession, they commit a criminal offence. However, they may defend their actions if they can prove that the non-compliance was due to factors beyond their control.

3.6 Prohibition of Processions

Should the chief constable determine that, due to prevailing conditions in a specific locality, imposing conditions on the procession would not suffice to avert serious public disorder, they possess the authority to seek a prohibition on all processions or those of a particular nature for up to three months.

(a) **In regions of England** (excluding London) and Wales, the chief constable must request this prohibition from the respective local council.

(b)   **Within the City of London and the broader London area,** the request is to be directed to the Secretary of State.

Committing to organise, knowingly taking part in, or inciting others to participate in a prohibited procession constitutes a legal offence.

4. Regulation of Public Assemblies

Public assemblies, much like public processions, are governed by a similar framework of regulations. A public assembly is considered to be a gathering of two or more individuals in a public space that is either entirely or partly exposed to the elements.

If the senior police officer holds a reasonable belief that a public assembly:

(a) **That is currently taking place or is intended,** could lead to significant public disorder, substantial property damage, or serious disruption to community life; or

(b) **Has been planned with the objective of intimidating others to compel them** either to perform an action they have the right to abstain from or to refrain from an action they have the right to undertake;

Then the senior police officer has the authority to issue directives to the individual coordinating or participating in the assembly as deemed essential to avert such disorder, damage, disruption, or intimidation. Nonetheless, any imposed condition must be justifiable and not excessively broad, in order to be aligned with the intended objectives.

4.1 Offences Related to Public Assemblies

If an organiser or participant of an assembly knowingly disobeys any conditions set by the police or incites others to the same, they are committing an offence, unless they can demonstrate that the breach was beyond their control.

4.2 Prohibitions on Trespassory Assemblies

Trespassory assemblies are characterised as gatherings that:

(a)   Consist of **at least 20 participants;**

(b)   Take place on private land where **public access is non-existent or severely restricted**;

(c)   Are likely to proceed **without the landowner's consent** or exceed any given consent or public access rights; and

(d)   Are anticipated **to significantly disrupt com-
      munity life** or cause considerable harm to land or
      structures of historical, architectural, or scientific
      significance.

Should the chief police officer of the region anticipate
the occurrence of such an assembly, they may approach
the local council to request a prohibition on all corresponding trespassory assemblies. Within the City of London and the broader London area, such requests are directed to the Home Secretary.

This legislation has a broad impact. It not only pertains
to sites of cultural significance like Stonehenge but also
encompasses gatherings that could impede traffic on public roads. This is due to the fact that a person's rights on a
public highway are limited to passing, repassing, and other reasonable activities.

Imagine a scenario where a group of environmental activists
gather within a fenced-off private field next to a busy motorway to protest against the construction of a new roadway
through an ancient forest.

The land is privately owned, and the group has neither
sought nor obtained permission to enter and assemble there.
The protest leads to significant traffic disruption as drivers
slow down to observe, causing tailbacks on the motorway.

Given the circumstances, the chief police officer fears that
the protest could escalate, leading to greater disruption and
potentially causing safety issues for both protestors and
drivers.

They may then request the local council to issue a ban on
such trespassory assemblies for a specified period, thereby
preventing the group from continuing their assembly on the
private land and mitigating the risk of serious disruption or
potential damage to the area.

(a) **Legal Consequences for Trespassory Assemblies.** Organising, participating in, or encouraging others to join a known banned trespassory assembly is illegal.

(b) **Authority to Prevent Attendance at Banned Assemblies.** Police officers are empowered to intercept and direct individuals they reasonably suspect to be en route to a banned assembly, instructing them not to proceed. Non-compliance with such a police directive constitutes an offence.

CHAPTER 11. POSITION OF THE EUROPEAN UNION IN THE UK CONSTITUTIONAL FRAMEWORK

1. European Union

1.1 Organisational Structure

The accession of the UK to the European Economic Community, which has evolved into the European Union (EU), marked a significant shift in its constitutional framework.

The EU operates under its principal agreements, the Treaty on European Union (TEU) and the Treaty on the Functioning of the European Union (TFEU), which confer its competences and outline the roles of its principal institutions:

(a) **European Council**—comprises the heads of state or government from each member nation.

(b) **Council of the European Union**—also known as the Council of Ministers, convenes in various formations depending on the policy domain, such as agriculture or transport. Ministers from member states with relevant portfolios participate, possessing the mandate to make decisions on their nation's behalf.

(c) **European Commission**—constitutes a commissioner from every member state, collectively forming the EU's executive arm. They are tasked with policy formulation as directed by the treaties and proposing legislative measures when necessary.

(d) **European Parliament**—consists of MEPs elected from each member state, sharing legislative responsibilities with the Council of the European Union, including sanctioning and amending legislative proposals.

(e) **Court of Justice of the European Union (CJEU)**—serves as the definitive interpreter of EU legislation. Primarily, it provides guidance on EU law to national courts through the preliminary ruling procedure, after which the domestic courts resolve the case with the now elucidated aspect of EU law.

1.2 Policy Domains

The EU's core mission has been to establish a single market that permits the unimpeded flow of goods, services, people, and capital across its member states, fostering economic prosperity through a larger, integrated market.

To accomplish this, harmonised regulations across the EU mitigate trade barriers and ensure that products and services can be exchanged without undue restrictions.

Besides the single market, the EU's policy reach extends to competition law, agriculture, fisheries, and a customs union, which facilitates collective trade negotiations with external nations.

2. EU Legislation

2.1 Foundational Treaties

The foundational treaties of the EU, namely the TEU and TFEU, lay down the fundamental regulations governing the EU. They define the jurisdiction and objectives of the EU's institutions, for instance, endorsing the principle of free trade and a shared approach to agriculture. These treaties represent the sole source of primary legislation within the EU framework.

2.2 Subordinate Legislation

Subordinate legislation, devised by the EU institutions (namely the Council of the European Union, European Parliament, and initiated by the European Commission), comprises the secondary legislative framework. This includes regulations and directives that offer detailed legislative measures to attain the broader aims set forth in the treaties.

(a) **Regulations.** EU regulations hold immediate legal force across member states and are directly enforceable without the need for additional national legislation.

(b) **Directives.** EU directives are binding upon the member states in terms of the outcomes to be achieved, yet they afford national governments the discretion to decide how to implement these objectives within their domestic legal systems.

2.3 Supremacy Principle

One of the cardinal principles established by the jurisprudence of the CJEU is the primacy of EU law. This doctrine asserts that EU law, as articulated in the treaties, regulations, and directives, takes precedence over the national laws of member states.

This requires that in instances of conflict between national law and EU law, national courts must uphold EU law. Justification: The efficacy of the EU's objectives hinges on the uniform application of EU law throughout all member states.

Should member states have the liberty to contravene EU law by enacting conflicting domestic laws, the authority of EU law would be significantly undermined.

2.4 Principle of Direct Effect

The principle of direct effect is a fundamental tenet of EU law whereby certain provisions of EU legislation may be invoked by individuals within member state courts without the necessity for transposition into national law.

This principle applies when EU provisions engender rights which national courts are bound to uphold.

For EU law to be directly effective, it must satisfy two criteria:

(a) **Clarity and precision** – The EU provision must be explicit and detailed, leaving no leeway for member states in terms of application or enactment; and

(b) **Unconditionality** – The implementation of the provision must not be subject to the discretion or further action of any public authority.

The rationale for the principle of direct effect is to prevent member states from nullifying the force of EU law by failing to integrate it within their domestic legal frameworks.

3. European Communities Act 1972

3.1 Incorporation of EU Laws into UK Law

With the UK's entry into the EU in 1973, the European Communities Act 1972 ('ECA 1972') was established, integrating EU law into the UK legal framework.

This Act ensured that legally binding EU laws, such as regulations and treaty provisions that are directly effective, were automatically incorporated into UK law.

Moreover, the ECA 1972 empowered the UK government to transpose EU directives into domestic law using secondary legislation, and occasionally through enacting primary legislation.

The forthcoming diagram will illustrate the interplay between UK domestic law and EU law as facilitated by the ECA 1972.

3.2 Establishment of EU Law Supremacy

The European Communities Act 1972 not only incorporated EU law into the UK legal system but also affirmed its supremacy.

The Act mandated that all existing or future UK legislation must be interpreted and applied in a manner consistent with EU law as adopted under the ECA 1972.

This adherence to the principle of supremacy meant that any UK legislation, whether enacted prior to or subsequent to the ECA 1972, would only remain valid if it was in accordance with EU law.

4. Brexit

A member state has the right to exit the EU, as stipulated by the Treaty on European Union, by notifying the European Council of its intention.

Following this protocol, the UK informed the European Council of its intention to withdraw in 2017. Subsequently, the UK Parliament enacted the European Union (Withdrawal) Act 2018, which led to the revocation of the European Communities Act 1972.

The UK also reached a Withdrawal Agreement that outlined the conditions of its departure from the EU, which took effect on 31 January 2020, marking the official exit of the UK from the EU.

5. The Brexit Transition Framework

The Withdrawal Agreement established a 'transition period' to facilitate a smoother separation following the UK's departure from the EU. During this period, the UK continued to adhere to EU rules and regulations, although it was no longer a member state.

This phase was designed to allow for the adjustment of citizens, businesses, and public administrations to the post-Brexit reality. The Agreement also included provisions safeguarding the residency and employment rights of EU citizens in the UK and reciprocal rights for UK nationals living in the EU.

6. European Union (Withdrawal) Act 2018 and the European Union (Withdrawal Agreement) Act 2020

6.1 EU Law Continuation During Transition

In light of the UK's withdrawal from the EU, the European Union (Withdrawal Agreement) Act 2020 ensured that, during the transition period, EU law remained applicable within the UK despite its formal departure from the Union.

This stipulation meant that until the end of the transition period on 31st December 2020, the UK would continue to be treated for most purposes as though it were still a member state.

6.2 Preservation of EU Law Post-Transition

The European Union (Withdrawal) Act 2018 was pivotal in retaining EU law within the UK legal system beyond the transition period.

This Act effectively preserved EU legislation as it stood immediately before the transition period concluded, converting it into a new category of domestic law called 'retained EU law'.

6.3 Types of Retained EU Law

The retained EU law encompasses several specific forms:

(a) **Section 2: EU-Derived Domestic Legislation.** Under Section 2 of the 2018 Act, all secondary legislation that had been introduced to transpose EU directives into UK law was safeguarded as 'EU-derived domestic legislation'.

This preservation also extends to any primary legislation passed for the purpose of enacting EU directives into UK law, such as the Equality Act 2010, which consolidated four different EU directives into one comprehensive Act. Post-Brexit, these laws continue to hold the same legal status they possessed prior to the UK's exit from the EU.

Consequently, secondary legislation created under the auspices of the ECA 1972 for the implementation of directives remains classified as secondary legislation, just as it did before the UK's departure from the EU. This principle equally applies to primary legislation.

(b) **Section 3: Direct EU Legislation.** As stipulated in Section 3 of the 2018 Act, all EU regulations, which were intrinsically binding and directly applicable in member states without the need for any national legal enactment, were in jeopardy of becoming defunct in the UK with the cessation of the transition period. To avert this legal vacuum, the 2018 Act transferred these EU regulations into the corpus of UK law, where they are henceforth recognised as 'direct EU legislation'. This legislative move ensured the continuity and effect of these regulations within the UK's legal framework post-Brexit.

(c) **Section 4: Directly Effective EU Law.** Previously, certain elements of EU law, including specific treaty articles, possessed direct effect, empowering individuals to invoke them in domestic courts without additional legislative measures. With the severance of the UK's formal ties to EU law at the close of the transition period, such provisions risked obsolescence. To prevent this, the 2018 Act safeguarded these EU law elements, maintaining them within the UK legal system as 'directly effective EU law', thereby ensuring their continued relevance and applicability.

(d) Section 5: Supremacy in Retained EU Law.
The 2018 Act continues to uphold the dominance of retained EU law over domestic UK law that predates the transition period's conclusion. Hence, in instances of conflict, the retained EU law takes precedence. Nevertheless, this supremacy does not extend to UK legislation passed subsequent to the transition period, granting the UK the autonomy to legislate in divergence from previously established EU law.

(e) Section 7A: Supremacy and Direct Effect in the Withdrawal Agreement. The Withdrawal Agreement meticulously tackles various critical issues stemming from the UK's departure from the EU, notably concerning the rights of EU citizens. Consequently, the UK and EU concurred that the doctrines of predominance and direct effect would govern the Withdrawal Agreement.

Therefore, according to Section 7A, any UK legal provisions that conflict with or are incompatible with the Withdrawal Agreement are to be overridden by the Agreement. Furthermore, any stipulations within the Withdrawal Agreement are granted direct effect, provided they align with the criteria established for EU law, namely being clear, precise, and unconditional.

Accordingly, whilst EU law ceases to be paramount in its entirety, the principles of supremacy and direct effect associated with EU law will persist in this confined context.

(f) **Section 6: Interpretation of Retained EU Law.** Beyond the scope of the Withdrawal Agreement, the courts in the UK are not obligated to adhere to any principles or rulings issued by the CJEU following the termination of the transition period. Rather, the courts may consider CJEU decisions as influential precedents.

Nonetheless, judgments from the CJEU and UK courts rendered before the transition period concluded are critical when addressing issues pertaining to the interpretation, legality, or implications of retained EU law, collectively termed 'retained case law'.

- **Retained EU Case Law versus Retained Domestic Case Law:** Retained case law encompasses two distinct groupings. Concerning retained EU law, the judgments of the CJEU constitute the 'retained EU case law' category, while the rulings of the UK's domestic courts constitute the 'retained domestic case law' category. This distinction is pivotal because retained EU case law obligates all domestic courts except the Supreme Court.

The Supreme Court retains the discretion to diverge from retained EU case law if deemed appropriate. This discretion mirrors the Supreme Court's capacity to depart from its own prior rulings. Retained domestic case law does not enjoy any particular privilege, meaning that apart from the Supreme Court, courts are bound by precedents from higher or equivalent courts within the hierarchy.

For instance, the High Court must follow decisions of the Court of Appeal, whereas the reverse is not required.

(g) **Section 7: Status of Retained EU Law.** Following the conclusion of the transition period, retained EU law was integrated as a specific category within the domestic legal framework. Notwithstanding this integration, UK law has the capacity to either revoke or modify retained EU law.

(h) **Section 8:** Addressing Withdrawal Deficiencies. The necessity to revise retained EU law stems from its initial drafting for the EU member states' context, which may lead to operational discrepancies due to the UK's departure from the EU. To this end, the 2018 Act empowers the government to create secondary legislation to rectify 'deficiencies' in retained EU law that stem from the withdrawal and hinder effective governance.

This **authority** encompasses:

- **Adjusting** provisions of retained EU law that are obsolete or lack practical relevance to the UK;

- **Reallocating** functions previously designated to EU entities that no longer hold relevance for the UK;

- **Establishing** reciprocal arrangements between the UK and the EU, as well as among the UK and other member states;

- **Instituting** other collaborative frameworks between the UK and EU that were contingent on the UK's EU membership; and

- **Updating** references to the EU that are deemed inapplicable.

Limitations on Rectifying Regulations:

Generally, these corrective regulations can implement any changes that would be within the scope of an Act of Parliament and can transfer functions from an EU institution to a UK public authority.

Nevertheless, **such regulations are constrained from:**

- Instituting or escalating taxes;

- Enacting retrospective provisions;

- Establishing criminal offences;

- Founding new public authorities; or

- Modifying or revoking the Human Rights Act, the Scotland Act 1998, the Northern Ireland Act 1998, or the Government of Wales Act 2006.

The authority to issue these regulations will lapse at the end of 2022.

(i) **Section 12: Devolved Legislatures and Retained EU Law.** Post-Brexit, the Scottish Parliament, Welsh Parliament, and Northern Ireland Assembly have gained the capacity to legislate in areas previously under EU law, provided they fall within their devolved competencies.

They can also modify or discard retained EU law within their jurisdiction unless UK government regulations specifically restrict this action.

Limitations on UK Government Regulations:

The UK government's power to issue regulations that limit the devolution legislatures' ability to alter retained EU law will expire two years after the transition period concludes. Regulations enacted under this provision remain in effect for five years from their effective date. After this period, the devolved legislatures regain the capacity to revise or nullify the retained EU law previously safeguarded by these regulations.

CONCLUSION

As we conclude this detailed exploration of Constitutional and Administrative Law and EU Law, essential for preparing the Solicitors Qualifying Examination (SQE 1), we reflect on the rich tapestry of legal principles, frameworks, and the evolving dynamics within these fields.

This guide has journeyed through the foundational aspects of the UK's constitutional mechanisms, delved into the complexities of administrative law, and navigated the multifaceted relationship between UK and EU legislation.

REFERENCES

Bradley, A.W., K.D. Ewing. (2022). Constitutional and Administrative Law. 18th ed. Pearson Education.

Loveland, I. (2021). Constitutional Law, Administrative Law, and Human Rights: A Critical Introduction. Oxford University Press.

Craig, P. (2015). UK, EU and Global Administrative Law: Foundations and Challenges. Cambridge University Press.

Barnett, H. (2017). Constitutional & Administrative Law. 12th ed. Routledge.

Brazier, R. (1999). Constitutional Practice: The Foundations of British Government. Oxford University Press.

Giussani, E. (2008). Constitutional and Administrative Law. Sweet & Maxwell.

Pollard, D., Parpworth, N., Hughes, D. (2007). Constitutional and Administrative Law: Text with Materials. Oxford University Press.

ABOUT AUTHORS

Anastasia & Andrew Vialichka have authored a revered collection of study guides and quizzes (metexam.co.uk), addressing the full spectrum of topics tested by the Solicitors Qualifying Examination (SQE).

Their portfolio encompasses thorough treatments of *Business Law and Practice, Dispute Resolution, Contract, Tort, Legal System of England and Wales, Constitutional and Administrative Law and EU Law, Legal Services, Property Law and Practice, Wills and the Administration of Estates, Solicitors Accounts, Land Law, Trusts, Criminal Law and Practice,* as well as *Equity.*

The authors' works are not only informational but also innovative, incorporating AI-based technology to enhance test preparation. This modern approach tailors learning to individual styles, aiding students to master both the theory and practice required for the SQE.